The World's Best Worst Jokes

By Rich Skinner

The World's Best Worst Jokes

Copyright © 2010 by Rich Skinner

ISBN: 978-0-557-70751-5

Dedicated to my wife, who would say to me,
"You're so funny, you should write a book"

Dear readers,

These are some of the lamest jokes I have heard, read, remembered or repeated to others.

Some of them are even funny.

With an added bonus of the dreaded 'Tis bottle joke

Enjoy. Rich Skinner

The book is divided into the following sections:

Riddles - pages 7 thru 13,

Lawyers - pages 14 thru 16,

Animals - pages 17 thru 21,

Christmas - pages 22 thru 24,

Yo Mamma - pages 25 thru 26,

Daffy-nitions - pages 27 thru 30,

Rednecks- pages 31 thru 35,

Signs- pages 36 thru 37,

Bumper stickers - 38 thru 42,

Ponderisms- pages 43 thru 50,

Confucius says- pages 51 thru 52,

Limericks- page 53,

Doctors- pages 54 thru 58,

Women - pages 59 thru 66,

Men - pages 67 thru 79,

Religious- pages 80 thru 93,

Ethnic- pages 94 thru 100,

Blondes- pages 101 thru 109,

Old Age- pages 110 thru 116,

You Know You're Getting Old - pages 117 thru 119,

Children- pages 120 thru 129,

with an added bonus of the dreaded 'Tis bottle joke - pages 130 thru 131.

Riddles

Q. What is big, red and eats rocks?
A. A big red rock eater.

Q. What is pink and fluffy?
A. Pink fluff

Q. What is blue and fluffy?
A. Pink fluff holding its breath.

Q. What is Smurf sex?
A. Doing it 'till your blue in the face.

Q. How do prisoners talk to each other?
A. With cell phones.

Q. Why did the man put his money in the freezer?
A. He wanted cold hard cash.

Q. Why did the boy throw the clock out the window?
A. Because he wanted to see time fly.

Q. Why did the toilet paper roll down the hill?
A. To get to the bottom.

Q. How do you tell when sour cream goes bad?
A. It begins to taste good.

Q. Why don't cannibals eat clowns?
A. They taste funny.

Q. What do you call cheese that's not yours?
A. Not cho cheese.(nacho)

Knock, Knock

Q. Who's there?
A. Nobody
Q. Nobody who? …Nobody who?

Q. Did you hear about the man who went into a full service gas station and asked for a dollars worth of gas?
A. The attendant sprayed the gas behind the man's ears.

Q. What is the advantage of electing a women president?
A. Think of all the money we can save by paying her less.

Q. What is the disadvantage of electing a women president?
A. It means another bush in the white house.

Q. Did you hear about the gay Mountie?
A. He always got his man.

Q. Did you hear about the guy who got a Viagra pill stuck in his throat?
A. Now he has a stiff neck.

Q. What is the shortest sentence in the English language?
A. No.

Q. What is the longest sentence?
A. I do.

Q. Which way did the computer thieves go?
A. They went data way.

Q. How can you keep milk from turning sour?
A. Keep it in the cow.

Q. What do you call a person who keeps on talking when people are no longer interested?
A. A boss.

Q. What's the difference between the Pope and your boss?
A. The Pope only expects you to kiss his ring.

Q. How do you top a car?
A. You tep on the brake, tupid.

Q. Why do women close their eyes during sex?
A. Because they hate to see a guy have a good time.

Q. Why is quitting smoking, like joining a nudist camp?
A. Because you don't know what to do with your hands.

Q. What did the leper say to the prostitute?
A. Keep the tip.

Q. What did the leper say to the prostitute?
A. I'm glad I don't have what you have.

Q. What do you call a prostitute with a runny nose?
A. Full.

Q. How can you tell if a woman is frigid?
A. Spread her legs. If a light comes on....

Q. What do you do if your nose goes on strike?
A. You pick-it.

Q. Where do 1-legged ladies work?
A. IHOP.

Q. What do you call a woman with 1 leg longer than the other?
A. Eileen.

Q. What do you call a woman with no legs?
A. Consuelo.

Q. What do you call a man with no arms and no legs?
A. Matt.

Q. What do you call a man with no arms and no legs going over a fence?
A. Homer.

Q. What do you call a man with no arms and no legs in the ocean?
A. Bob.

Q. Does England have a 4th of July?
A. Yes, and a 5th and a 6th, too.

Q. How many months have 28 days?
A. All of them.

Q. Why is 6 afraid of 7?
A. Because 7 ate 9.

Q. If April showers bring May flowers, what do May flowers bring?
A. Pilgrims.

Q. What do clouds wear under their clothes?
A. Thunderwear.

Q. What goes in hard and straight and comes out soft and mushy?
A. Chewing gum.

Q. What does a pool table and a man's trousers have in common?
A. Pockets.

Q. What is long, round and full of seamen?
A. A submarine.

Q. What is small but has something large between its legs?
A. A jockey.

Q. What is 6.9?
A. 69 interrupted by a period.

Q. What is 68?
A. That's when you tell the girl to do you, and you'll owe her one.

Q. Why is pubic hair so curly?
A. Because if it was straight, it would poke your eye out.

Q. What are the small bumps around a woman's nipples for?
A. It's Braille for 'suck here'.

Q. What is an Australian kiss?
A. It's the same as a French kiss, but 'down under.'

Q. What do you do with 365 used condoms?
A. Melt them down, make a tire, and call it a good year.

Q. What is black and white and red all over?
A. A nun falling down the stairs.
A. A newspaper

Q. What is black and white with a cherry on top?
A. A police car.

Q. How do you keep a moron in suspense?
A. I'll tell you tomorrow.

Q. What do you call a boomerang that doesn't come back?
A. A stick.

Q. What is a soldier's favorite date?
A. March 4th.

Q. If you're Italian in the kitchen and French in the bedroom, what are you in the bathroom?
A. European.

Q. How many men does it take to clean a bathroom?
A. None. That's women's work.

Q. What do you tell a woman with 2 black eyes?
A. Nothing, you've already told her twice.

Q. Where do sick ships go?
A. The doc.

Q. What is the quietest sport?
A. Bowling, because you can hear a pin drop.

Q. When is a door not a door?
A. When it's ajar.

Q. If there were 4 potatoes in a room, which one would be the prostitute?
A. The one that's labeled 'I DA HO'.

Q. How do you separate the men from the boys in a gay bar?
A. With a crowbar.

Q. How did Helen Keller's parents punish her when she was bad?
A. They left a plunger in the toilet.

Q. How can you tell if a woman is ticklish?
A. Give her a test-tickle.
Q. Did you hear about the new perfume that drives women wild?
A. It smells like money.

Q. Why do woman like Wonton soup?
A. Because wonton spelled backwards is not now.

Q. How many computer techs does it take to change a light bulb?
A. One. To tell you, 'Turn the switch off, now turn it back on. Is it still broken?'

Q. How many computer programmers does it take to change a light bulb?
A. None. That's hardware.

Q. What happens if you fart in church?
A. You sit in your own pew.

Q. If you were dying, what would you do?
A. I'd go into the living room and eat a life saver.

Q. Which sense diminishes with age?
A. The sense of decency.

Q: Why were all hurricanes formerly named after women?
A: Because when they arrive, they're wild and wet.
   But when they go, they take your house and car with them.

Q. What is a the ultimate embarrassment for a man?
A. Running into a wall with an erection and breaking his nose.

Lawyers

Q. How can you tell if a lawyer is lying?
A. His lips are moving.

Q. What do you call 100 lawyers buried up to their necks?
A. A good start.

Q. What is the difference between a dead lawyer in the middle of the road and a dead skunk in the middle of the road?
A. There are brake marks in front of the skunk.

A court appointed lawyer was defending a client in lower court.
The judge found him guilty and said, "30 days and $30.00."
The lawyer asked his client, "What do you want to do?"
The client said, "Lets appeal it upstairs."
The lawyer said, "Your honor, we appeal this case to a higher court."
When they appealed the higher court, the judge said, "60 days and $60.00."
The lawyer asked his client, "What do you want to do now?"
The client brightened and said, Lets appeal it back down stairs."

A policeman was being cross-examined by a defense attorney during a trial.
The lawyer was trying to undermine the policeman's credibility.
The lawyer asked, "Officer, did you see my client fleeing the scene?"
The officer responded, "No sir, But I observed a person matching the description of the offender running several blocks away."
The lawyer asked, "Who provided the description?"
The officer responded, "The officer who responded to the scene."
The lawyer pressed, "A fellow officer provided the description. Do you trust your fellow officers?"
The officer replied, "Yes sir. With my life"
The lawyer then asked, "With your life? Let me ask you this. Do you have a room where you change clothes in preparation for your daily duties?"
The officer replied, "Yes sir. We do!"
The lawyer then asked, "And do you have a locker in the room?"
The officer replied, "Yes sir. I do"
The lawyer then asked, "And do you have a lock on that locker?"
The officer again replied, "Yes sir. I do"
The lawyer then asked, "Why is it, if you trust your fellow officer with your life, you find it necessary to lock your locker in a room you share with these men?"
The officer replied, "You see, we share the building with the court complex, and sometimes lawyers have been known to walk through that room."

A Mafia Godfather finds out that his bookkeeper has cheated him out of 5 million bucks.

His bookkeeper is deaf. That was the reason he got the job in the first place. It was assumed that the bookkeeper would hear nothing that he might have to testify about in court.

When the Godfather goes to confront the bookkeeper about his missing $5 million, he takes along his lawyer who knows sign language.

The Godfather tells the lawyer, "Ask him where the 5 million bucks is that he embezzled from me."

The lawyer, using sign language, asks the bookkeeper where the money is.

The bookkeeper signs back, "I don't know what you are talking about."

The lawyer tells the Godfather, "He says he doesn't know what you are talking about."

The Godfather pulls out a pistol, puts it to the bookkeeper temple and says, "Ask him again!"

The lawyer signs to the bookkeeper, "He'll kill you if you don't tell him."

The bookkeeper signs back, "OK. You win! The money is in a brown briefcase, buried behind the shed in my cousin Bruno's backyard in Woodbridge!"

The Godfather asks the lawyer, "What did he say?"

The lawyer replies, "He says you don't have the balls to pull the trigger."

The Supreme Court has ruled that there cannot be a Nativity Scene in the nations Capital this Christmas. It's not for religious reasons, they just can't find 3 wise men and a virgin.

"Mr. Smith, I have reviewed your case, the divorce judge said, And I've decided to give your wife $500 a week."

"That's more than fair, your honor,", said the husband. "And every now and then I'll try to send her some money too."

An attorney boarded an airplane in New Orleans with a box of frozen crabs and rudely told the flight attendant to take care of them. He also told her that he was holding her personally responsible for the crabs staying frozen and mentioned that he was a lawyer

and ranted about what would happen to her if she let them thaw out.

The flight attendant stowed the box of crabs, but was extremely upset over how his behavior and how she was treated.

When the plane finally touched down, she got on the intercom and announced to the entire cabin, "Would the man who gave me crabs in New Orleans, please raise your hand?"

An investment broker was looking for a lawyer and started interviewing them. She started off by saying, "As you can understand, in this type of business our integrity must be beyond question. So tell me, are you an honest lawyer?"

The lawyer replied, "Honest? Let me tell you about my honesty. Why, I am so honest, that my father lent me twenty thousand dollars for my education and I paid him back every penny the minute I tried my first case."

The broker was impressed, and said, "That's impressive. What type of case was it?"

The lawyer squirmed a bit and finally said, "It was my Father. He was suing me for the money"

A man was chosen for jury duty who really did not want to serve and tried to get himself dismissed from serving. He tried every thing he could think of to get him self excused but nothing seemed to work. As the trial was about to start, he asked if he could approach the bench.

He starts, "You honor, I should be excused from this trial because I am prejudiced against the defendant. I can take one look at him sitting over there in the grey suit with those beady eyes and know he is guilty. Look at that dishonest face. He's a crook! He's guilty!

So your honor, I should be excused from this trial. I can not possibly stay on this jury."

To which the judge exclaimed, "Get back in the jury box, you idiot. The man your describing is the defendants lawyer."

A man walks into a bar with an alligator under his arm and asks the bartender, "Do you serve lawyers here?"

"I sure do", relies the bartender.

"Good. Give me a beer and give the alligator a lawyer" said the customer.

Animals

Q. Why don't ducks fly upside down?
A. Because they would quack up.

Q. What do ducks eat with their soup?
A. Quackers.

Q. Why don't dogs make good dancers?
A. Because they have 2 left feet.

Q. What type of dogs can tell time?
A. Watch dogs.

Q. What do you call a dog with no legs?
A. Nothing. He can't come anyway.

Q. Why do they have elections in November?
A. So we can pick a turkey.

Q. Why did the elephant cross the road?
A. It was the chicken's day off.

Q. Why did the chicken cross the road?
A. It was the Colonel's day off.

Q. Why did the coyote cross the road?
A. To get the chicken.

Q. Why did the chicken cross the playground?
A. To get to the other slide.

Q. How did the pig get to the hospital?
A. By hambulance.

Q. Why do hummingbirds hum?
A. Because they don't know the words.

Q. What did one horse say to the other horse?
A. Why the long face.

Q. Where do cows hang their art work?
A. In a moosuem.

Q. What did the boy octopus say to the girl octopus?
A. Can I hold your hand, hand, hand, hand, hand, hand, hand, hand?

Q. What does a frog order at McDonalds?
A. Flies and a croak.

Q. What is green and red and goes around in a circle?
A. A frog in a blender.

Q. What is gray and comes in quarts?
A. An elephant.

Q. Why did the elephants go on strike?
A. They were tired of working for peanuts.

Q. What do you get when you cross an elephant with a rhino?
A. El-if-I-know.

Q. How do you stop a rhino from charging?
A. Take away his credit card.

Q. What do you get when you cross a centipede with a turkey?
A. I don't know what you call it, but everybody gets a drumstick.

Q. Where do skunks go to college?
A. P.U.

Q. How do snails settle their differences?
A. They slug it out.

Q. How do you make an elephant float?
A. You start with 2 scoops of elephant and some root beer.

Q. What did one doe say to the other doe?
A. Why don't we go into town and blow a few bucks?

Q. What do you get when you cross a pickle and a deer?
A. A Dil-do.

Q. What is Smokey the Bear's middle name?
A. The.

Q. What did one mouse say to the other mouse?
A. Come around the corner and I'll show you my hole.

Q. Do you know how to make a chicken omelet?
A. You take the egg out of the chicken, then turn around and put the chicken into the egg.

Q. What is worse than finding a worm in an apple?
A. Finding half a worm. A. Finding a worm in your poop.

Q. Why don't lobsters like to share?
A. Because they're shellfish.

Q. Why are fish so smart.
A. Because they travel in schools.

Q. Why don't Ostriches and Penguins fly?
A. Because they can't get past airport security.

Q. What did one flea say to the other flea?
A. Should we walk or take the dog?

Q. Why didn't the butterfly go to the ball?
A. Because it was a moth ball.

A farmer bought a new stud rooster for his henhouse one day.
The new rooster struts over to the old rooster and says, "Ok old timer. It's time for you to retire. I'm the new stud here"
The old rooster replies, "Surely you can't handle all the chickens. Can't you just let me have the two old hens in the corner?"
The young rooster replies, "Scram, You're over the hill and I'm taking over"
The old rooster says, "Tell you what. I'll race you around the farmhouse. Whoever wins will get to be the exclusive stud for the hen house."
The young rooster laughs at him and says, "You don't stand a chance."
The old rooster says, "How about if you give me a 5 second head start. That should keeps things fair between us."
The young rooster says, "You're on!"
The old rooster takes off running towards the farmhouse. 5 seconds later the young rooster is taking off after him. They round the front porch of the farmhouse and the young rooster is closing the gap on the old rooster, while the old rooster is running and squawking as fast and as loud as he can. The farmer hears all the noise, comes out on the porch, grabs his rifle, aims and BOOM!
He blows the young rooster to bits.
Shaking his head he mutters, "That's the 3rd gay rooster they sold me this month!"

If a penguin is found dead on the ice, the other penguins will dig holes in the ice with there wings and beaks, until the hole is big enough for the dead bird. Then the other penguins will roll the dead penguin into the hole, cover it back up, gather in a circle around the fresh grave and start singing, "Freeze a jolly good fellow..."

A papa mole, a mama mole, and a baby mole, all live together in a little mole hole.
One day, papa mole sticks his head out of the hole, sniffs the air and says, "Yum! I smell maple syrup!"
The mama mole sticks her head out of the hole, sniffs the air and said, "Oh, Yum! I smell honey!"
Now baby mole is trying to stick his head out of the hole to sniff the air, but can't because the bigger moles are in the way.
This makes him whine and he states, "Gee, all I can smell is MOLASSES!"

Two veterans were talking when the first one says to the other, "Do you know that Elks have sex 5 times a day?"
The second one says, "Damn, and we joined the VFW!"

If you make a cow laugh, does milk come out its nose.

The early bird may get the worm, but the second mouse gets the cheese in the trap.

Did you ever eat a cured ham and wonder what it had?

If a pig stops grunting, does that make it disgruntled?

How do dead bugs wind up in an enclosed light fixture?

Never try to baptize a cat.

I taught my parrot to say, "Tastes like chicken"

Dog is my co-pilot.

You can't trust dogs to watch your food.

Why when you blow in a dog's face, he gets mad at you, but when you take him for a car ride, he sticks his head out the window?

I got a dog for my wife. An excellent trade.

The more I understand women, the more I like my dog.

I taught my dog to play classical music on the piano, now his Bach is worse than his bite.

If we evolved from apes, why are there still apes?

A baby seal walked into a club…

Christmas

Q. Did you hear about the dyslexic devil worshiper?
A. He sold his soul to Santa.

Q. What do Santa Claus and a dog have in common?
A. They both leave something under a tree.

Q. What is it called if you are afraid of jolly men in red suit?
A. Santa Claustrophobia.

Q. Why doesn't Santa Claus have kids?
A. Because he only comes once a year .

Q. Why does Santa Claus go down the chimney?
A. Because it soots him.

Q. What does Santa Claus like to do in his garden?
A. He likes to hoe, hoe, hoe.

Q. What do you get if you deep fry Santa Claus?
A. Krispy Cringle.

Q. What nationally is Santa Claus?
A. North Polish.

Q. Who brings Christmas presents to a police station?
A. Santa Clues.

Q. Why does Santa have to be a man?
A. No woman would wear the same outfit year after year

Q. Why does Santa wear red underwear?
A. Because he did all his laundry in one load.

Q. Why is Christmas like working in an office?
A. You do all the work and the fat guy in the suit gets all the credit.

Q. Who sings "Blue Christmas" and makes toy guitars?
A. Elfis.

Q. How many elves does it take to change a light bulb?
A. Ten. One to change the light bulb and nine to stand on each others shoulders.

Q. What doe elves learn in school?
A. The elf-abet and elf control.

Q. Why was Santa's helper depressed?
A. Because he had low elf esteem.

Q. What do you call Santa's helpers?
A. Subordinate Clauses.

Q. How long do an elf's legs need to be to be considered an elf?
A. They need to reach the ground.

Q. What are the 3 stages of life?
A. You believe in Santa Claus, you don't believe in Santa Claus, you look like Santa Claus.

Q. If athletes get athletes foot, what do astronauts get?
A. Missile toe.

Q. What's the difference between a snow man and a snow woman?
A. Snow balls.

Q. What do snowmen eat for breakfast?
A. Snowflakes.

Q. What do you get when you cross a snowman with a vampire?
A. Frostbite.

Q. What was it that made Frosty the Snowman come to life?
A. It was the snow blower, not the old silk hat as previously thought.

Q. Why do all the other reindeer have brown noses?
A. Because they can't stop as fast as Rudolph.

Yo Momma

Yo momma's so fat, her ass has its own zip code.

Yo momma's so fat, her ass has a moon.

Yo momma's so fat, her belt is the equator.

Yo momma's so fat, her toothpick is a cane.

Yo momma's so fat, she puts make-up on with a paint roller.

Yo momma's so fat, when kids yell Kool-Aid, she crashes thru a wall.

Yo momma's so fat when she wears a yellow raincoat, people said "Taxi!"

Yo momma's so fat she had to go to Sea World to get baptized

Yo momma's is so fat, the last time she went to the Twin Towers, they collapsed.

Yo momma's so poor she can't afford to pay attention!

Yo momma's so lazy she's got a remote control just to operate her remote!

Yo momma's so old that when she was in school there was no history class.

Yo momma's so ugly she made an onion cry!

Yo momma's so ugly just after she was born, her mother said "What a treasure!" and her father said "Yes, let's go bury it."

Yo momma's so stupid it took her 2 hours to watch 60 minutes.

Yo momma's so stupid she took the Pepsi challenge and chose Jif.

Yo momma's so hairy Bigfoot is taking her picture!

Yo momma's so nasty she brings crabs to the beach.

Daffy-nitions

Adult - someone who has stopped growing at both ends, but is growing in the middle.

Archeologist -Someone whose career is in ruins.

Bachelor - That's a guy who abides by life, liberty and the happiness of pursuit.

Barbell - something you ring in a bar.

Barium - What the undertaker does to you after you're dead.

Beauty Parlor - where women go to curl up and dye.

Benign - is what you will be after you be eight.

Cannibal - someone who is fed up with people.

C.E.O. - Chief Embezzlement Officer

Chicken - an animal that we eat before its born and after its dead.

Committee - that is a group of people that keeps minutes but wastes hours.

Defeat – it's what you put de-shoes on.

Defense – what you use de-feat to climb.

Dilate - not dying early

Dumbbell - not a smart bell.

Dust - mud with the water squeezed out

Earthquake - Topographical error

Fascinate - If you have a sweater with ten buttons, but you only fasten-eight.

Faux Pas - something for your father.

Foreclose - something to do with your clothes.

Gay – abbreviation for Got Aids Yet.

Gross - Two vampires fighting over a bloody tampon.

Hammer – tool used to locate the most expensive items next to what you are trying to hit.

Handkerchief - Cold storage.

H.M.O. - Have money? Operate.

Husband - Someone who, after taking the trash out, gives the impression that he just cleaned the whole house.

International Date Line - a place to call for dates.

Job – Just Over Broke.

Keyboard - that where you hang your keys.

Loser -That's someone who goes to a family reunion to meet women.

Mass Transit - Taking the bus to church.

Marriage - Finding the one person you are going to annoy for the rest of your life.

Mixed emotions - Seeing your mother-in-law drive your new car over a cliff.

Mosquito - an insect that makes you like flies.

Mouse pad - Where a bachelor mouse lives.

O.P.E.C. - Over Priced Energy Council.

Pap smear - To insult or belittle your father.

P.E.T.A - People Eating Tasty Animals.

Piece d' resistance- Girl that fights back.

Phillips Screwdriver – tool used for stripping heads off Phillips screws.

Pliers – Tool used to round off bolt heads.

P.M.S. - Punish My Spouse. also Prime Murder Suspect.

Prostitute - someone who can't whistle while they work..

Schmuck - That's someone who gets out of the shower to pee.

Secret - something you tell to one person at a time.

Shortcut - The longest distance between two points.

Slut - That's a woman with the morals of a man.

Software - plastic knives, forks and spoons.

S.P.A.M. - Something Posing As Meat.

Teenager - God's punishment...for enjoying sex.

Transvestite - That's a guy who likes to eat, drink and be Mary.

Tomorrow - the greatest labor saving device of today.

Tumor - not one more, but...

Utility knife – tool used to slice thru contents of cardboard boxes.

Wrinkles - something other people have but not you.

Rednecks

Q. What is the definition of Redneck?
A. That's someone who has been married more than once, and has the same in-laws.

Q. How do you know the toothbrush was invented by a Redneck?
A. Other wise it would have been called a 'teethbrush'

Q. Why is it so hard to solve a Redneck murder?
A. The DNA all matches, and there are no dental records.

Q. How do you know when you're staying in a Redneck motel?
A. When you call the front desk and say, "I gotta leak in my sink", and the clerk replies, "Well, go ahead."

Q. If a Redneck couple divorce, are they still cousins?
A. Only in Kentucky, Alabama, Arkansas and Georgia.

Q. Why did the Redneck bait his fishing pole with plutonium?
A. So he could go nuclear fishin.

Q. What are the only two things a Redneck handy man uses?
A. Duct tape and WD-40.
If its not supposed to move and it does, use the duct tape.
If its supposed to move and doesn't, use to WD-40.

Did you hear why they raised the minimum drinking age for Rednecks to 32?
They want to keep alcohol out of the high schools.

There is a new $3 million Redneck Lottery.
The winner gets $3.00 a year for a million years.

A Redneck passed away and left his entire estate to his beloved widow ...
but she can't touch it 'til she's 16.

A State Trooper pulls over a pickup and says to the driver, "Got any I.D.? "
and the driver replies "Bout wut?"

Redneck Security System:

1. Buy a pair of used men's boots.

2. Place on porch along with a copy of Guns & Ammo.

3. Put giant dog dishes next to boots and magazine.

4. Leave note on door that says:

Don't mess with the pit bulls!
They attacked the mailman this morning and messed him up real bad.
I think he'll be OK, but there was sooo much blood.
Anyway, I locked them all in the house. Be back real soon.

Two rednecks were talking when one says to the other, "Say, why do them scuba divers always fall backwards off the boat into the water?"
The other one replied, "You dumbass, If the fell forward, they still be in the damn boat."

Two rednecks decided to get in on a raffle and each bought a ticket.
When the drawing came, the first redneck won a years supply of spaghetti.
His friend won a toilet brush. A couples of weeks passed and the two friends met.
The one asked the other, "How's that spaghetti you won?"
The other replied, "It's great. I love spaghetti. How's the toilet brush you won?"
The first one replied, "Not so good. I think I'm gonna go back to using paper"

Two rednecks decided to go hunting. They are walking in the woods when one of them sits down to take a rest. After a few minutes he tells his friend, "I'm not feeling too good."
His friend asks, "Can you make it back to the truck?"
The first one says, "I think so."
The start walking back to the truck when the first redneck collapses.
The second redneck quickly takes out his cell phone and dials 911.
The operator answers, "911, what's your emergency?"
He replies, "My friend collapsed. He might have had a heart attack and I think he's dead. What do I do?"
The operator replies, "Well first make sure he's dead."
The guy says ,"OK."
A second later the 911 operator hears a loud BANG!
The guy gets back on the line and says, "OK, he's dead, now what?"

A redneck went fishing in his one day but ran out of worms. He saw a cottonmouth slithering around by the shore with a frog in its mouth and heard that frogs make good bait. Figuring the snake couldn't bite him with a frog in its mouth, he grabbed the snake right behind the head, and took the frog. Now he didn't know how to release the snake without it biting him. He decides to grabs his bottle of Jack Daniels and pours a little whiskey in the snakes mouth. The snakes eyes rolled back in its head, and he went limp.
The redneck released him into the lake and went about fishing. A little while later, he felt a gentle nudge on his foot. He looked down and saw the snake with 2 frogs in its mouth.

While driving across country, a man stops at a gas station in a little redneck town.
Thinking he was close to crossing into the next time zone, he asks the attendant, "Do you know when does the time change?"
The attendant replies "Sometime in October, I reckon."

A lady arrived at a car dealership to pick up her car and was told her keys had been locked in it. Going to the service department she found a redneck mechanic working feverishly to unlock the driver side door.
As she watched from the passenger side, she instinctively tried the door handle and discovered that it was unlocked.
"Hey," she announced to the redneck mechanic, "its open!"
He replied, "I know. I already got that side."

A redneck took his wife to a restaurant. The waiter took his order first.
"I'll have the strip steak, medium rare", he said.
The waiter asked, "Aren't you worried about the mad cow?"
"Nah, she can order for herself", he replied.

A wife asked her redneck husband if a certain dress made her butt look big.
He told her not as much as the dress she wore yesterday.

A redneck asked his wife, "Where do you want to go for our anniversary?"
"Somewhere I haven't been in a long time!" she said.
So he suggested, "How about the kitchen?"

When the redneck got home from work, his wife demanded that he take her someplace expensive... so, he took her to a gas station.

A wife was hinting about what she wanted for her upcoming anniversary to her redneck husband.

She said, "I want something shiny that goes from 0 to 160 in about 3 seconds." So he bought her a scale.

A hiring manager at a Wal-Mart in Tennessee, had the task of hiring someone to fill a job opening. After sorting through a stack of 20 resumes he found four people who were equally qualified. The manager decided to call the four in and ask them only one question. Their answer would determine which of them would get the job. The day came and as the four sat around the conference room table, the manager asked, "What is the fastest thing you know of?"

The first man replied, "A thought. It just pops into your head. There's no warning."

"That's very good!" replied the manager.

"And now you sir?" he asked the second man.

"Hmmm....let me see. A blink! It comes and goes and you don't know that it ever happened. A blink is the fastest thing I know of."

"Excellent!" said the manager. "The blink of an eye, that's a popular cliché for speed".

He then turned to the third man, who was contemplating his reply.

"Well, out at my dad's ranch, you step out of the house and on the wall there's a light switch. When you flip that switch, way out across the pasture the light on the barn comes on in less than an instant. Yup, turning on a light is the fastest thing I can think of."

The manager was very impressed with the third answer and thought he had found his man.

"It's hard to beat the speed of light," he said.

Turning to Bubba, the fourth and final man, the manager posed the same question.

Old Bubba replied, "After hearing the previous three answers, it's obvious to me that the fastest thing known is DIARRHEA."

"WHAT!?" said the manager, stunned by the response.

"Oh sure", said Bubba. "You see, the other day I wasn't feeling so good, and I ran for the bathroom, but before I could THINK, BLINK, or TURN ON THE LIGHT, I had already shit my pants."

One year a redneck decided to buy his mother-in-law a cemetery plot as a Christmas gift. The next year he didn't buy her a gift.

When she asked him why, he replied "You still haven't used the gift I bought you last year!"

A man calls the garage door repair company for a broken garage door. A redneck repairman shows up, examines the door and tells the man that one of the problems is that he did not have a large enough motor on the opener. The man replied, "I have the largest one Sears makes, a 1/2 horsepower." The redneck shook his head and said, "You need a 1/4 horsepower." The man responded with, "1/2 is larger than 1/4. The redneck repairman responded with, "NO, it's not. Four is larger than two..."

A redneck woman was mixing up batter to bake her children a cake. When she was finished, her redneck son asked, "Can I lick the bowl?" To which his mother said, "No, flush it like everyone else."

Signs

Sign at a Radiator repair shop:
"Best place to take a leak"

Sign on door to maternity ward:
"Push, Push, Push"

Sign on a fence:
"Salesman welcome. Dog food is expensive"

Sign at a Veterinary waiting room:
"Sit. Stay"

Sign at a Travel agency:
"Please go away"

Sign at a Gynecologist's Office:
"Dr. Jones, at your cervix"

Sign at a Urologist's Office:
"Please hold"

At a Proctologist's office:
"To expedite your visit please back in."

On an Electrician's truck:
"Let us remove your shorts."

At the Electric Company:
"We would be *de-lighted* if you send in your payment.
If you don't, you will be."

At a Tire Shop:
"Invite us to your next blowout"

At a Brake Shop:
"Stop in… if you can"

In front of a Funeral Homes:
"Our day begins when your day ends"
"Drive carefully. We're in no rush to see you"

At a truck stop:
"Eat here and get gas"

At a body repair shop:
"We take the dent out of acci-dent"

At a tennis court:
"Tennis…What a racquet"

At a fish market:
"Get your crabs here"

At a bowling alley:
"Bowling…It's right up your alley"

At a country store:
"If we don't have it, you don't need it"

On a property sign:
"Trespassers will be shot, survivors will be shot again"

On an RV:
"RV there yet?

On a dirty car window:
"Test dirt. DO NOT Remove"

In front of a prison:
"Do Not Stop to Pick Up Hitchhikers"

On church marquees:
"We need to talk-God"
"Be humble or you'll stumble"
"Heaven-it's a gated community"
"God doesn't believe in Atheists"
"Our church is prayer conditioned"
"CH_RCH - All that's missing is U"
"Don't make me come down there-God"
"Don't wait till your dead to go to church"
"Give Satan an inch and he'll be your ruler"
"You can either go to church or you can go to Hell"
"Have you read my No. 1 best seller. There will be a test-God"
"Laying in bed, screaming 'Oh God', does not count as going to church"

On bumper stickers:

You say bitch like it's a bad thing.

From zero to witch in …Poof!

My wife's other car is a broom.

Witches parking. All others will be toad.

My other car is a pair of boots.

What would Scooby Doo?

Horn broken…watch for finger

Keep honking, I'm re-loading as fast as I can.

If you don't like the way I drive, stay off the sidewalk.

Not happy with the way I drive, dial 1-800-EAT SHIT.

Don't follow me, I'm lost.

Don't follow me, you won't make it.

Don't laugh, it's paid for.

My Karma ran over your Dogma.

I brake just to piss you off.

I am driving fast because I have to poop.

I'm driving this fast so I can get there before I forget where I'm going.

I'm not speeding, I'm qualifying.

If you are going to ride my ass… give me a kiss.

Watch my rear end, not hers.

As a matter of fact, I do own the damn road.

I have one nerve left, and you're getting on it.

No, this is NOT an abandoned vehicle.

My child can beat up your Honor roll student.

My inner child is a mean little f*cker.

Join the dark-side, they have cookies.

Do you believe in life after death? Mess with my truck and you'll find out.

I do whatever my Rice Krispies tell me.

I owe, I owe, it's off to work I go.

I might as well go to work, I'm already in a bad mood.

I'm not myself today, maybe I'm you.

I refuse to grow up and you can't make me.

I've never been this old.

I used up all my sick days, so I called in dead.

It used to be wine, woman and song. Now it's beer, the old lady and TV.

Ass, Gas, or Grass… Nobody rides for free.

Get in, Sit down, Hold on and Shut up.

Because I'm the princess, that's why.

51% Princess, 49% Bitch. Don't push me.

I am a bitch, just not yours.

Treat me like you would any queen.

My tastes are simple, I only want the best.

I'm not spoiled, I only want the best.

All we are saying is give peas a chance.

If you don't care what I have to say, why are you squinting to read this?

D.D.A.M.- Dyslexic Drivers Against Mothers

The worst day fishing/golfing is better than the best day at work.

I putt better than I drive.

But officer, I thought you wanted to race.

I want to be the person my dog thinks I am.

More wagging, less barking.

Déjà Moo: When you've heard this bull before.

Adult child from alien elders.

Things haven't been the same ever since that house fell on my sister.

Don't make me release the flying monkeys.

My next wife/husband is going to be normal.

I don't have A.D.D, it just that... Oh look a bunny.

My wife says I don't listen, or something like that.

I miss my ex, but my aim is improving.

I wake up with fear and terror every morning, but then I leave to go fishing.

Driver carries no cash, he's married.

I've taken a vow of poverty, to annoy me send money.

Girls just wanna have funds.

Never drive faster than your guardian angel can fly.

Atheism- myth understood.

Who would Jesus bomb?

I'd tell you to go to Hell, but I work there and don't want to see you everyday.

Don't blame me, I voted for…

Someone stole my support magnet.

For a good time, call someone else.

Amazingly, I don't give a crap.

I'm pretending to care.

Ask me about my ability to annoy complete strangers.

I'm smiling. That alone should frighten you.

Milk sucks, got Margaritas?

Paratroopers are good to the last drop.

Archers like to shoot the bull.

Welders like to heat thing up.

Entrepreneurs mind their own business.

It takes a lot of balls to play golf.

I'm a senior, my blinker is supposed to be on.

Eve was framed.

Well behaved women rarely made history.

It's a Jeep Thing, you wouldn't understand.

I got your 'Jeep Thing', now it burns when I pee.

Manwhore.

Here to all the kisses I've snatched and vice versa.

Save a horse - Ride a cowgirl.

Save a whale, harpoon a fat chick.

You're Momma is hot.

My other ride is your mom.

There is nothing like lipstick on your dipstick.

Will have sex for beer.

To all virgins… Thanks for nothing.

Ponderisms

To err is human, to really foul things up takes a computer.

I married Miss Right. Her first name's 'Always'.
Actually, her middle name's 'Always'. Her first name's 'Not'.

A day without sunshine is night.

If flying is so safe, why do they call the airport the terminal?

Why don't you ever see the headline 'Psychic Wins Lottery'?

On the other hand, you have different fingers.

42.7 percent of all statistics are made up on the spot.

74 percent of people don't believe in statistics.

There are 3 types of people in this world. Those that can do math, and those that can't.

99 percent of lawyers give the rest a bad name.

2 wrongs don't make a right, 3 lefts do.

If you can smile when things go wrong, you have somebody in mind to blame.

Half the people you know are below average.

I can't find Hidden Valley Ranch.

He who laughs last, thinks slowest.

Depression is merely anger without enthusiasm.

Families are like fudge. Mostly sweet, with a few nuts.

Stress is caused by 3 things: Money, family and family with no money.

Stressed spelled backwards is desserts.

Live within your means, even if you have to borrow to do it.

One good turn gets all the covers.

How come every holiday has a mattress sale?

Support bacteria. They're the only culture some people have.

Where exactly is the 'Any' key?

A clear conscience is usually the sign of a bad memory.

My mind not only wanders, it sometimes leaves completely.

Of all the things I lost, I miss my mind the most.

Change is inevitable, except from vending machines.

If you think nobody cares, try missing a couple of payments.

How many of you believe in psycho-kinesis? Raise my hand.

Politicians and diapers are changed for the same reason.

How come our oil is in Alaska, California, and Oklahoma, but all are dipsticks are in Washington D.C.

So what's the speed of dark?

When everything is coming your way, you're in the wrong lane.

Why is the shortest line, always the slowest moving?

Hard work pays off in the future. Laziness pays off now.

Never take a laxative and a sleeping pill on the same night.

Never pierce your tongue if you wear dentures.

Never wear a nose ring with bifocals.

How much deeper would the ocean be without sponges?

It used to be only death and taxes were inevitable. Now, there's shipping and handling.

I'd rather have a bottle in front of me than a frontal lobotomy.

What happens if you get scared half to death, twice?

I drink lite beer. It has half the calories so I can have twice as many.

Never bring beer to a job interview.

I get my Vitamin C from drinking beer with lime.

Why do psychics have to ask you your name?

Women are psychic. They know if we are going to get some before we do.

If its not one thing it's a mother.

I am in shape, round is a shape.

The only crunches I do are made by Nestle.

The only exercise I get is running after the ice cream truck.

The only exercise I get is running from the police.

I gain weight from eating my own words or swallowing my pride.

I gave up jogging when my thighs kept rubbing together and setting fire to my pants.

Why is a round pizza in a square box cut into triangles?

I used to eat a lot of natural foods until I learned that most people die of natural causes

Health nuts are going to feel stupid someday, lying in hospitals dying of nothing.

Forget the health foods, I need all the preservatives I can get.

Inside every older person is a younger person wondering, "What the heck happened?"

Light travels faster than sound. That's why some people appear bright until they speak.

I showed up early for my premature ejaculation meeting.

Who cares what other people think, they do it so infrequently.

Life isn't like a box of chocolates. It's more like a jar of jalapenos. What you do today, might burn your butt tomorrow.

I'd like to try day trading. I'd start by trading Mondays for Saturdays.

I read an article on the dangers of heavy drinking. It scared me so much that I said, "That's it! No more reading."

Why do we park on a driveway and drive on a parkway?

Why does your nose run and your feet smell?

Be true to your teeth, or they'll be false to you.

Avoid clichés like the plague.

When I die, I want to die like my grandfather--who died suddenly in his sleep. Not screaming like all the passengers in his car.

Can a hearse carrying a corpse drive in the carpool lane?

I have enough money to last the rest of my life as long as I don't buy anything.

I'm with the government; I'm here to help you.

If the opposite of 'Pro is 'Con, is the opposite of 'Progress-Congress'

For every action, there is an equal and opposite government program.

A penny saved is a government oversight.

So why do brain cells come and go, but fat cells live forever.

All the people who think they are perfect are annoying to us who are.

I thought I was mistaken, but I was wrong.

I used to be conceited, but now I'm perfect.

I used to be indecisive, but I'm not sure now.

I suffer from A.D. ... something.

I can keep a secret. It's the people I tell it to that can't.

I'm mad that I can't control my anger issues.

I could care less about your apathy.

I'm all for being spontaneous, as long as I plan for it ahead of time.

I'm all for volunteering as long as they pay me for it.

I'm bi-polar, but only half the time.

I'm not saying my wife is a bad cook, but the last time she cracked open an egg, a pair of stockings fell out.

I'm not saying my wife's a bad cook, but I pray after I eat.

Whenever I feel blue, I start breathing again.

Sometimes I think I understand everything, and then I regain consciousness.

If Jimmy cracks corn and no one cares, why is there a song about him?

No, I do not want fries with my baked potato.

The easiest way to find something lost around the house is to buy a replacement.

There are two kinds of pedestrians: the quick and the dead

If you look like your passport picture, you need the trip.

I was so ugly when I was born, the Doctor slapped my father.

Not having children is hereditary. If your parents didn't have kids, chances are you won't either.

Birthdays are good for you. The more you have, the longer you live.

They are going to start checking DMV and Post Office employees for drugs. They won't find speed.

If corn oil is made from corn, and vegetable oil is made from vegetables, what is baby oil made from?

If electricity comes from electrons, does morality come from morons?

Do illiterate people eat Alphabet Soup?

If a deaf person has to go to court, is it still called a hearing?

Why doesn't glue stick to the inside of the bottle?

Powdered water, just add water.

If an invisible man married an invisible woman, would their kids be anything to look at?

Why when I press 1 for English, I still can't understand the guy.

1 in 3 people are crazy. If it's not the one on your right, and not the one on your left....

4 out of 5 prisoners prefer gang rape.

Did you ever take a dump so big, you clothes fit better afterwards.

Why doesn't a bell pepper ring when you shake it?

If you rearrange the letters Mother-in-Law, it spells Woman Hitler.

Why are there no Father-In-Law jokes?

My twin brother forgot my birthday.

Why does a careless match start a forest fire, but it takes a whole box to start a camp fire?

How come the one who says 'Calm Down', is the one who got you mad in the first place.

Why is the International House of Pancakes located only in America?

I wondered why the baseball was getting bigger, and then it hit me.

Some mistakes are too much fun to only make once.

To write with a broken pencil is pointless.

Dead batteries were given out free of charge.

I dreamt I was a muffler and woke up exhausted.

I dreamt I drank a 5 gallon margarita, when I woke up my toilet bowl was empty and there was salt around the seat.

Why is the third hand on a clock or watch called the second hand?

How come when your alarm clock goes off, its really turning on.

How come 'after dark, really means 'after light'?

How come a 'strike' is a hit in bowling, but a miss in baseball.

When life hands you lemons, find somebody with Tequila, then add salt.

Coffee isn't my cup of tea.

My wife gives good headache.

My 4-leaf clover gave me a rash.

A broken vacuum cleaner sucks.

It's a recession when your neighbor loses his job; it's a depression when you lose yours.

Things are so bad, the mafia is laying off judges.

The road to success is always under construction.

Whoever said life is fair was cheating.

Why isn't there a sarcastic font?

Did Popeye eat Olive Oil with his Spinach?

I used to be a Gynecologist, but I ate up all my profits.

Confucius says:

Girl who fly upside down, have crack up.

Girl who go to mans apartment for late night snack, usually get tit-bit.

He who pull out too fast, leave rubber.

Man with hole in pocket, feel himself nutty.

Crowded elevator always smell different to midget.

Dumb man climb tree to get cherry, wise man spread limbs.

Man who lay woman on ground gets piece on earth.

Wise man never play leapfrog with unicorn.

Man who take sleeping pill and laxative on the same night will wake up in deep shit.

Man's wife his better half, his mistress his better whole.

Married man should forget mistakes. No use 2 people remembering same thing.

Woman worries about future, until she gets husband. Man not worried about future until he gets wife.

Wife not part of furniture, until screwed on bed.

Woman has last word in argument. Next word man say is beginning of new argument.

Successful man one who makes more money than wife can spend.
Successful woman is one who can find such a man.

Panties not best thing on earth, but next to it.

Girl who douches with vinegar, walk around with sour puss.

Boy who goes to bed with sex problem wake up with solution in hand.

He who hesitates, must change his underwear.

Man trapped in brothel get jerked around.

Don't sweat the petty stuff ... and don't pet the sweaty stuff.

Incestuous sisters are nibbling siblings.

Fast girls make slow wives.

Secretary who gets to big for job has been working too close to boss.

Girl who sleep with judge get honorable discharge.

Woman who screw on fence enjoys post position.

Pilot who masturbate in plane have hijack.

Man who hump donkey make ass of self.

He who kiss woman's ass have crack in jaw.

Beware, in some Chinese restaurants you may be eating pussy without knowing it.

Limericks:

There once was a man named Dave,
who kept an old whore in a cave.
She was ugly as shit,
and missing one tit,
but think of the money he'd save.

In four-teen hundred and ninety two,
Columbus sailed the ocean blue,
He hit a rock,
split his cock,
and pee'd all over the crew .

Old mother Hubbard,
went to her cupboard,
to fetch her poor dog a bone.
But when she bent over,
Rover took over,
cause he had a bone of his own.

A young schizophrenic named Struther,
Who learned of the death of his Brother,
Said, "I know that its bad,
But I don't feel too sad.
After all, I still have each other."

There once was a young man named Skinner,
who took a young lady to dinner.
At a quarter to nine,
they sat down to dine,
and at 9:45 it was in her.
(Skinner, not the dinner)

There once was a man named Tupper
Who took a young lady to supper
At a quarter to nine
They sat down to dine
At twenty to ten it was up her
Not Tupper, not supper
It was some sonofabitch named Skinner

Doctors

The doctor said, "Bill, the good news is I can cure your headaches.
The bad news is that it will require castration.
You have a very rare condition, which causes your testicles to press on your spine and the pressure creates one hell of a headache.
The only way to relieve the pressure is to remove the testicles."
Bill was shocked and depressed. He wondered if he had anything to live for.
He had no choice but to go under the knife.
When he left the hospital, he was without a headache for the first time in 20 years, but he felt like he was missing an important part of himself.
As he walked down the street, he realized that he felt like a different person.
He could make a new beginning and start a new life.
He saw a men's clothing store and thought, "That's what I need... a new suit."
He entered the shop and told the salesman, "I'd like a new suit."
The elderly tailor eyed him briefly and said, "Let's see... size 44 long."
Bill laughed, "That's right, how did you know?"
"Been in the business 60 years!" the tailor said.
Bill tried on the suit. It fit perfectly. As Bill admired himself in the mirror, the salesman asked, "How about a new shirt?"
Bill thought for a moment and then said, "Sure." The salesman eyed Bill and said, "Let's see 34 sleeves and 16-1/2 neck."
Bill was surprised, "That's right, how did you know?"
"Been in the business 60 years!"
Bill tried on the shirt and it fit perfectly. Bill walked comfortably around the shop and the salesman asked, "How about some new underwear?"
Bill thought for a moment and said, "Sure."
The salesman said, "Let's see... size 36."
Bill laughed, "Ah ha! I got you; I've worn a size 34 since I was 18 years old."
The salesman shook his head, frowning, "You can't wear a size 34.
A size 34 would press your testicles up against the base of your spine and give you one hell of a headache."

A doctor told his patient that he has good news and bad.
The good news is "We are going to name a disease after you."

A doctor told his patient that he had good news and bad.
"The good news is you only have 24hrs to live", said the Doctor.
"If that's the good news, what is the bad news?", the patient exclaimed.
"I tried to call you yesterday."

"I have some good news and some bad news", said the Doctor to his patient.
"The good news is, I'm going to buy that new BMW I've wanted.
The bad news is, you're going to pay for it."

A doctor told his patient that he has some bad news.
"Our test results came back. You have Cancer and Alzheimer's", says the
doctor.
The patient thinks a minute and replies," Well at least I don't have Cancer."

The phone rings and the lady of the house answers,
"Hello." "Mrs. Sanders, please."
"Speaking."
"Mrs. Sanders, this is Doctor Jones at Saint Agnes Laboratory. When your
husband's doctor sent his biopsy to the lab last week, a biopsy from another Mr.
Sanders arrived as well. We are not uncertain which one belongs to your
husband. Frankly, either way the results are not too good."
"What do you mean?" Mrs. Sanders asks nervously.
"Well, one of the specimens tested positive for Alzheimer's and the other one
tested positive for HIV. We can't tell which is which."
"That's dreadful! Can you do the test again?", questioned Mrs. Sanders.
"Normally we can, but Medicare will only pay for these expensive tests one
time."
"Well, what am I supposed to do now?"
"The folks at Medicare recommend that you drop your husband off somewhere
in the middle of town. If he finds his way home, don't sleep with him."

The man told his doctor that he wasn't able to do all the things around his
house that he used to do.
When the examination was complete, he said. "Now Doc, I can take it. Tell me
in plain English, what is wrong with me."
"Well in plain English, you're just lazy," the doctor replied.
"Okay", said the man, "Now tell me in medical terms so I can tell my wife."

American Medical Association researchers have found that:
Patients needing blood transfusions may benefit from receiving chicken blood
rather than human blood. It tends to make the men cocky and the women lay
better!

The last time I went to my Doctor, he wanted a sperm, urine and blood sample.
So I gave him my underwear.

The only cow in a small town in Arkansas stopped giving milk. The people did some research and found they could buy a cow up in Antigo, Wisconsin, for $200.

They bought the cow from Wisconsin and the cow was wonderful. It produced lots of milk all of the time, and the people were pleased and very happy. They decided to acquire a bull to mate with the cow and produce more cows like it. They would never have to worry about their milk supply again. They bought a bull and put it in the pasture with their beloved cow.

However, whenever the bull came close to the cow, the cow would move away. No matter what approach the bull tried, the cow would move away from the bull and he could not succeed in his quest.

The people were very upset and decided to ask the Vet, who was very wise, what to do.

They told the Vet what was happening. "Whenever the bull approaches our cow, she moves away. If he approaches from the back, she moves forward. When he approaches her from the front, she backs off. An approach from the side and she walks away to the other side", they said.

The Vet thinks about this for a minute and asked, "Did you buy this cow in Wisconsin?"

The people were dumbfounded, since they had never mentioned where they bought the cow. "You are truly a wise Vet," they said.

"How did you know we got the cow in Wisconsin?"

The Vet replied with a distant look in his eye, "My wife is from Wisconsin."

Five surgeons are discussing who makes the best patients on the operating table. The first surgeon says, "I like to see accountants on my operating table, because when you open them up, everything inside is numbered."

The second responds, "Yeah, but you should try electricians! Everything inside them is color coded."

The third surgeon says, "No, I really think librarians are the best; everything inside them is in alphabetical order."

The fourth surgeon chimes in: "You know, I like construction workers...those guys always understand when you have a few parts left over at the end, and when the job takes longer than you said it would."

But the fifth surgeon shut them all up when he observed: "You're all wrong. Politicians are the easiest to operate on. There's no guts, no heart, and no spine, and the head and butt are interchangeable."

A 60 year old man recently picked a new primary care doctor. After two visits and exhaustive Lab tests, the doctor said he was doing 'fairly well' for his age. A little concerned about that comment, he couldn't resist asking him, "Do you think I'll live to be 80?"

The doctor asked, "Do you smoke tobacco, or drink beer or wine?"

"Oh no," he replied. "I'm not doing drugs, either!"

Then the doctor asked, "Do you eat rib-eye steaks and barbecued ribs?"

He said, "Not much... my former doctor said that all red meat is very unhealthy!"

"Do you spend a lot of time in the sun, like playing golf, sailing, hiking, or bicycling?"

"No, I don't," he said.

The doctor asked, "Do you gamble, drive fast cars, or have a lot of sex?"

"No," the man said.

He looked at the man and said, "Then why do you even give a shit?"

A man is recovering from surgery when the nurse comes in and ask how he is feeling.

"I'm ok, but I didn't like the four letter word the doctor used in the surgery."

"What word was that?" the nurse asked.

"Oops!" he replied.

A male patient is lying in bed in the hospital, wearing an oxygen mask over his mouth and nose, still heavily sedated from a difficult four hour surgical procedure.

A young student nurse appears to give him a partial sponge bath.

"Nurse," he mumbles from behind the mask, "Are my testicles black yet?"

Embarrassed, the young nurse replies, "I don't know, sir. I'm only here to wash your upper body."

He struggles to ask again, "Nurse, are my testicles black yet?"

Concerned that he may elevate his vitals from worry about his testicles, she overcomes her embarrassment and sheepishly pulls back the covers. She raises his gown, holds his penis in one hand and his testicles in the other, lifting and moving them around and around gently.

Then she takes a close look and says, "'No sir, they aren't and I assure you, there's nothing wrong with them!"

The man pulls off his oxygen mask, smiles at her and says very slowly,

"Thank you very much. That was wonderful, but listen very, very closely -

"Are-my-test-results-back-yet?"

A doctor examining a woman who had been rushed to the Emergency Room, took the husband aside, and said, "I don't like the looks of your wife at all."
"Me neither doc," said the husband.
"But she's a great cook and really good with the kids."

A woman goes to the doctor, beaten black and blue.
The doctor asks, "What happened?"
The woman replies, "Doctor, I don't know what to do. Every time my husband comes home drunk he beats me to a pulp."
The doctor says, "I have a real good cure for that. The next time your husband comes home drunk, just take a glass of sweet tea and start swishing it in your mouth. Just swish and swish but don't swallow until he goes to bed and is asleep."
Two weeks later the woman comes back to the doctor looking fresh and reborn.
The woman says, "Doctor, that was a brilliant idea! Every time my husband came home
drunk, I swished with sweet tea. I swished and swished, and he didn't touch me!"
The doctor states, "You see what happens when you keep your mouth shut?"

Women

A sexy woman went up to the bar in a quiet rural pub. She gestured alluringly to the bartender who approached her immediately. She seductively signaled that he should bring his face closer to hers.

As he did, she gently caressed his full beard. "Are you the manager?" she asked, softly stroking his face with both hands.

"Actually, no," he replied.

"Can you get him for me? I need to speak to him," she said, running her hands beyond his beard and into his hair.

"I'm afraid I can't," breathed the bartender. "Is there anything I can do?"

"Yes. I need for you to give him a message," she continued, running her forefinger across the bartender's lips and slyly popping a couple of her fingers into his mouth and allowing him to suck them gently.

"What should I tell him?" the bartender managed to say.

"Tell him," she whispered, "there's no toilet paper, hand soap, or paper towels in the ladies room."

Two ladies talking in heaven:

1st woman: Hi! My name is Wanda.

2nd woman: Hi! I'm Kelly. How'd you die?

1st woman: I Froze to Death.

2nd woman: How Horrible!

1st woman: It wasn't so bad. After I quit shaking from the cold, I began to get warm & sleepy, and finally died a peaceful death. And you?

2nd woman: I died of a massive heart attack. I suspected that my husband was cheating, so I came home early to catch him in the act. But instead, I found him all by himself in the den watching TV.

1st woman: So, what happened?

2nd woman: I was so sure there was another woman there somewhere that I started running all over the house looking. I ran up into the attic and searched, and down into the basement. Then I went through every closet and checked under all the beds. I kept this up until I had looked everywhere, and finally I became so exhausted that I just keeled over with a heart attack and died.

1st woman: Too bad you didn't look in the freezer---we'd both still be alive.

A couple is lying in bed.

The man says, "I am about to make you the happiest woman in the world"

The woman says, "I'll miss you…"

Once upon a time, a long time ago, there was a woman.

She didn't whine, nag, bitch or complain.

It was a long time ago, and it was only once.

A little girl asked her Mother, "Where did we come from?"
Her mother replied, "God made Adam and Eve and they made all the people of the world."
The little girl then asked her Dad, "Where did we come from?"
Her father replied, "We evolved from monkeys."
The girl goes back to her mother, "Dad told me we came from monkeys; you told me we came from Adam and Eve. Which is true?"
Her mother says, "I told you about my side of the family, he told you about his."

A woman went to a pet shop and immediately spotted a large, beautiful parrot. There was a sign on the cage that said $50.00.
"Why so little," she asked the pet store owner.
The owner looked at her and said, "Well, I should tell you first, that this bird used to live in a house of prostitution and sometimes it says some pretty vulgar stuff."
The woman thought about this, but decided she wanted the bird any way.
She took it home, hung the bird's cage up in her living room and waited for it to say something.
The bird looked around the room, then at her, and said, "New house, new madam."
The woman was a bit shocked at the implication, but then thought 'that's not so bad.'
When her teenage daughters returned from school, the bird looked at them and said, "New house, new madam, new girls."
The girls and the woman were a bit offended but then began to laugh about it. considering how and where the parrot had been raised.
Soon after, the woman's husband came home from work.
The bird looked at him and said, "Hi Keith!"

A man bumps into a woman in a hotel lobby and as he does, his elbow goes into her breast. They are both quite startled.
The man turns to her and says, "Ma'am, if your heart is as soft as your breast, I know you'll forgive me."
She replies, "If your penis is as hard as your elbow, I'm in room 221."

A couple drove down a country road for several miles, not saying a word. An earlier discussion had led to an argument and neither of them wanted to concede their position.
As they passed a barnyard of mules, goats, and pigs, the husband asked sarcastically, "Relatives of yours?"
"Yep," replied the wife, "in-laws."

Three women, one engaged, one married, and one a mistress, are chatting about their relationships and decide to amaze their men. That night all three will wear a leather bodice S&M style, stilettos and mask over their eyes.
After a few days they meet again.
The engaged girlfriend said, "The other night, when my fiancée came back home, he found me in the leather bodice, 4" stilettos and a mask.
He said, "You are the woman of my life, I love you." Then we made love all night long."
The mistress stated: "Oh yes! The other night we met in his office. I was wearing the leather bodice, mega stilettos, mask over my eyes and a raincoat. When I opened the raincoat, he didn't say a word. We just had wild sex all night."
The married one then said, "The other night I sent the kids to stay at my mother's for the night. I got myself ready, leather bodice, super stilettos and mask over my eyes. My husband came in from work, fell in his mangy Lazy-boy, grabbed the TV controller and a beer, and said, "Hey Batman, what's for dinner?"

A little old lady is walking down the street dragging two large plastic garbage bags behind her. Noticing this, a policeman stops her, and says, "What are you dragging in those bags"
The little old lady says, "You see, my back yard is right next to the football stadium parking lot. On game days, a lot of fans come and pee through the fence into my flower garden. So, I stand behind the fence with my hedge clippers. Each time some guy sticks his pecker through the fence, I say, '$20 or off it comes."
"Well, that seems only fair.' laughs the cop. Oh, what's in the other bag?"
"Well, you know", says the little old lady, "not everybody pays."

A man walks into a Bank, gets in line, and when it was his turn he pulls out a gun and robs the Bank!
Just to make sure he leaves no witnesses, he turns around and asks the next customer in line: "Did you see me rob this Bank?"
The customer replies ....."Yes"
The bank robber raises his gun points it to the customer head and BANG!!!!... Shoots the customer in the head and kills him!
The bank robber quickly moves to the next customer in line and says to the woman: "Did you see me rob this bank????"
The woman calmly responds, "No ... but my husband did!"

A man and his wife were having some problems at home and were giving each other the silent treatment. Suddenly, the man realized that the next day, he would need his wife to wake him at 5:00 AM for an early morning business flight.
Not wanting to be the first to break the silence (and LOSE), he wrote on a piece of paper,
"Please wake me at 5:00 AM." He left it where he knew she would find it.
The next morning, the man woke up, only to discover it was 9:00 AM and he had missed his flight. Furious, he was about to go and see why his wife hadn't wakened him, when he noticed a piece of paper by the bed. The paper said, "It is 5:00 AM. Wake up."

A man said to his wife one day, "I don't know how you can be soo stupid and soo beautiful all at the same time."
The wife responded, "Allow me to explain. God made me beautiful so you would be attracted to me; God made me stupid so I would be attracted to you!"

One Saturday morning, an avid fisherman got up early, dressed quietly, made his lunch, grabbed his fishing gear, slipped quietly into the garage, loaded up to the truck, and proceeded to back out into a torrential down pour.
The wind was blowing 50 mph. He pulled back into the garage, turned on the radio, and discovered that the weather would be bad throughout the whole day. He went back into the house, quietly undressed, and slipped back into bed.
There he cuddled up to his wife's back, now with a different anticipation, and whispered, "The weather out there is terrible."
His loving wife of 20 yrs replied, "Can you believe my stupid husband is out fishing in that?"

A man breaks out of prison and breaks into a home where a husband and wife are having breakfast. The prisoner ties up both of them, then whispers something to the wife.
She whispers something back and he leaves the room.
The husband says, "Look at that guy. He is all dirty and disgusting, and he's wearing prison clothes. He must have just broken out of. He probably hasn't been with a woman in a long time. Be strong, I love you. What did he whisper to you?"
The wife says "He said he is gay, thought you are cute and wants to know where we keep the Vaseline. I told him the bathroom. Be strong, I love you too."

A couple couldn't decide what to give their mailman for a Christmas present. The next day the mailman shows up at the door with a package. The wife takes the package from him, and brings him inside. Then she starts kissing him, undressing him and leading him into the bedroom. When they finish, she gets her purse and gives him a dollar.

He looks at it and asks her, "What is this for?"

The wife replies, "My husband and I couldn't decide what to give you for a Christmas tip, so he said, 'Ahh, Screw him, give him a dollar'."

Mike was going to marry Karen so Mike's Father sat him down for a little chat. He said, "Mike, let me tell you something. On my wedding night in our honeymoon suite, I took off my pants, handed them to your Mother, and said, 'Here - try these on'."

She did and said, "These are too big. I can't wear them."

I replied, "Exactly. I wear the pants in this family and I always will and ever since that night, we have never had any problems."

"Hmmm," said Mike. He thought that might be a good thing to try.

On his honeymoon, Mike took off his pants and said to Karen, "Here, try these on."

She tried them on and said, "These are too large. They don't fit me."

Mike said, "Exactly. I wear the pants in this family and I always will. I don't want you to ever forget that."

Then Karen took off her panties and handed them to Mike.

She said, "Here you try on mine."

He did and said, "I can't get into your panties."

Karen said, "Exactly. And if you don't change your smart-ass attitude, you never will."

The seven dwarfs of menopause:

Itchy, Bitchy, Sweaty, Sleepy, Bloated, Forgetful and Psycho

A woman calls her boss one morning and tells him that she is staying home because she is not feeling well.

"What's the matter?" he asks.

"I have a case of anal glaucoma," she says in a weak voice.

"What the heck is anal glaucoma?" he wants to know.

"I can't see my ass coming into work today."

A woman is standing nude, looking in the bedroom mirror.

She is not happy with what she sees and says to her husband, "I feel horrible; I look old, fat and ugly. I really need you to pay me a compliment."

The husband replies, "Your eyesight's damn near perfect."

A woman who was a tree hugger and an anti-hunter purchased some land. There was a large tree on one of the highest points. She wanted a good view of the natural splendor of the land so she started to climb the big tree. As she neared the top, she encountered a large owl that attacked her. In trying to escape she slid down the tree and got splinters in her crotch. In considerable pain, she made her way to the nearest doctor, where she explained that she was an environmentalist and how she came to get the splinters. The doctor listened and told her to wait in the examining room and he would be with her shortly. 4 hours later the doctor finally entered the examining room.

The woman was angry and demanded, "What took you so long?"

The doctor told her, "I sorry it took so long. I had to get permits from the Environmental Protection Agency, US Forestry Service and the Bureau of Land Management before I could remove old growth timber from a recreational area."

A couple were struggling to make ends meet and the husband decided his wife should be a prostitute to make some extra money.

She asked him, "What do I do?"

He relied, "Dress provocatively, stand outside on the corner and wait for a car to stop."

After some time standing there, a car finally stops. She tells the driver to wait a minute and runs inside to her husband.

She tells him, "A car stopped. Not what should I do?"

The husband replies, "Tell him you'll gave him sex for $100 dollars."

She runs back to the car and says, "You can have sex with me for $100 dollars."

The driver checks his wallet and says, "I don't have $100, what can I get for $30?"

She tells the driver to wait a minute and runs inside to her husband.

She tells her husband, "He doesn't have 100, and wants to know what he can get for 30."

The husband thinks a minute and says, "Tell him you give him a hand job for $30."

She runs back out the car tells the driver, "For $30, you can have a hand job."

The driver agrees, gives her the money and unzips his pants. He then unrolls his giant, enormous, thick shlong of a penis.

She tells the driver to wait a minute and runs inside to her husband.

Getting inside, she blurts out, "Honey, can I borrow 70 dollars?"

An old woman is riding in an elevator in a very lavish New York City building when a young, beautiful woman gets into the elevator, smelling of expensive perfume. She turns to the old woman and says arrogantly, "Romance" by Ralph Lauren, $150 an ounce!"

Then another young and beautiful woman gets on the elevator, and also very arrogantly turns to the old woman saying, "Chanel No. 5, $200 an ounce!"

About three floors later, the old woman has reached her destination and is about to get off the elevator.

Before she leaves, she looks both beautiful women in the eye, then bends over, squeezes one off and says, "Broccoli - 49 cents a pound!"

After retiring, a man went to the Social Security office to apply for Social Security. The woman behind the counter asked him for his driver's license to verify his age. He looked in his pockets and realized he had left his wallet at home. He told the woman that he was very sorry, but he would have to go home and come back later.

The woman said, "Unbutton your shirt."

So he opened his shirt revealing his curly silver hair.

She said, "That silver hair on your chest is proof enough for me" and she processed his Social Security application.

When he got home, he excitedly told his wife about the experience at the Social Security office.

She said, "You should have dropped your pants. You might have gotten disability, too."

A man and wife were sitting at a table at his high school reunion.

He kept staring at a drunken lady swigging her drink as she sat alone at a nearby table.

His wife asked, "Do you know her?"

"Yes," he sighed, "She's my old girlfriend. I understand she took to drinking right after we split up those years ago, and I hear she hasn't been sober since."'

"My God!" says the wife, "Who would think a person could go on celebrating that long?"

A man and a woman were asleep like two innocent babies.

Suddenly, at 3 o'clock in the morning, a loud noise came from outside.

The woman, bewildered, jumped up from the bed and yelled at the man "Holy crap. That must be my husband!"

So the man jumped out of the bed; scared and naked jumped out the window.

He smashed himself on the ground, ran through a thorn bush and to his car as fast as he could

A few minutes later he returned and went up to the bedroom and screamed at the woman, "I AM your husband!"

The woman yelled back, "Yeah, then why were you running?"

On a cross country airplane flight, shortly after take off, the Captain announces over the loudspeaker, "Thank you for flying with our airlines, we will be flying at 35,000 feet, at a cruising speed of 525 mph, and we will arrive in California in 5 hrs."

He then adds, "5 hours? I'm beat. I could sure use a cup of coffee and a blowjob."

One of the stewardess runs up to the cockpit to tell the captain that his mike is still on.

Seeing the stewardess, one of the passengers yells out, "Don't forget the coffee!"

Men

A man walks into a restaurant with a full-grown ostrich behind him.
The waitress asks them for their orders.
The man says, "A hamburger, fries and a coke," and turns to the ostrich, "What's yours?"
"I'll have the same," says the ostrich.
A short time later the waitress returns with the order "That will be $9.40.,"
The man reaches into his pocket and pulls out the exact change for payment.
The next day, the man and the ostrich come in again and the man says, "I'll have a hamburger, fries and a coke."
The ostrich says, "I'll have the same."
Again the man reaches into his pocket and pays with exact change.
This becomes routine until the two enter again. "The usual?" asks the waitress.
"No, this is Friday night, so I will have a steak, baked potato and a salad," says the man.
"Same," says the ostrich.
Shortly the waitress brings the order and says, "That will be $32.62."
Once again the man pulls the exact change out of his pocket and places it on the table.
The waitress cannot hold back her curiosity any longer. "Excuse me, sir. How do you manage to always come up with the exact change in your pocket every time?"
"Well," says the man, "several years ago I was cleaning the attic and found an old lamp. When I rubbed it, a Genie appeared and offered me two wishes. My first wish was that if I ever had to pay for anything, I would just put my hand in my pocket and the right amount of money would always be there."
"That's brilliant!" says the waitress. "Most people would ask for a million dollars or something, but you'll always be as rich as you want for as long as you live!"
"That's right. Whether it's a gallon of milk or a Rolls Royce, the exact money is always there," says the man.
The waitress asks, "What's with the ostrich?"
The man sighs, pauses and answers, "My second wish was for a tall chick with a big butt and long legs who agrees with everything I say."

A man walks into his bedroom to find his wife in bed with his best friend.
Turning to his friend he say, "Bill, I have to, but you?"

My credit card was stolen recently, but I didn't report it.
It seems the crook was charging less than my wife.

Maude and John, both 81, lived in The Villages, in Florida. They met at the singles club meeting and discovered over time that they enjoyed each other's company.

After several weeks of meeting for coffee, John asked Maude out for dinner and, much to his delight, she accepted. They had a lovely evening. They dined at the most romantic restaurant in town. Despite his age, they ended at his place for an after-dinner drink. Things continued along a natural course and age being no inhibitor, Maude soon joined John for a most enjoyable roll in the sack. As they were basking in the glow of the magic moments they'd shared, each was lost for a time in their own thoughts.

John was thinking: "If I'd known she was a virgin, I'd have been gentler."
Maude was thinking: "If I'd known he could still do it, I would have taken off my pantyhose."

An elderly couple was on a cruise and it was really stormy. They were standing on the back of the boat watching the moon when a wave came up and washed the old woman overboard. They searched for days and couldn't find her, so the captain sent the old man back to shore with the promise that he would notify him as soon as they found something.

Three weeks went by and finally the old man got a fax from the boat. It read: "Sir, sorry to inform you that we found your wife dead at the bottom of the ocean. When we hauled her on deck we found an oyster attached to her rump with a pearl in it worth $50,000."

The old man faxed back: "Send me the pearl and re-bait the trap."

A man owned a small farm in Iowa. The State Wage and Hour Department claimed he was not paying proper wages to his help and sent an agent out to interview him.

"I need a list of your employees and how much you pay them," demanded the agent.

"Well, there are my hired hands. One has been with me for four years; the other for three. I pay them each $600 a week, plus free room and board. The cook has been here for 18 months, and I pay her $500 a month plus free room and board.

"Then there's the half-wit that works here about 18 hours a day. He takes home $10 a week and I buy him a bottle of bourbon every week to keep him going," said the farmer.

"That's the guy I want to talk to: the half-wit," said the agent.

The farmer said, "That would be me."

My wife keeps saying I am a dirty old man.
I keep telling her I'm not that old.

A man and his wife, now in their 60's, were celebrating their 40th wedding anniversary.

On their special day a good fairy came to them and said that because they had been such a devoted couple, she would rant each of them a very special wish.

The wife wished for a trip around the world with her husband. Woosh! Immediately she had airline and cruise tickets in her hands. The man wished for a female companion 30 years younger…Whoosh!… Immediately he turned 90!

A man rushes home, sits down in front of the TV and yells out to his wife, "Honey get me a beer before it starts."

She brings him a beer. He opens it and drinks it while watching the TV.

A few minutes later he yells out to his wife," Honey, get me another beer before it starts."

She brings him a beer. He opens that one it and drinks it while watching the TV.

He yells out again," Honey get me another beer before it starts."

At this point the wife gets annoyed stating," Are you just going to sit there drink beer and watch television. No conversation? No how was your day?"

To which the husband states," Damn! It started."

A man was to be hanged for telling bad jokes.

Upon sentencing, the judge said to the man, "If you promise not to tell any more dumb jokes, I won't hang you."

The man replied," No noose is good noose", and they hung him.

Young Chuck moved to Texas and bought a donkey from a farmer for $100.00. The farmer agreed to deliver the donkey the next day.

The next day he drove up and said, "Sorry son, but I have some bad news, the donkey died."

Chuck replied, "Well, then, just give me my money back."

The farmer said, "Can't do that. I went and spent it already."

Chuck said, "Ok, then, just bring me the dead donkey."

The farmer asked, "What ya gonna do with him?"

Chuck said, "I'm going to raffle him off."

The farmer said, "You can't raffle off a dead donkey!"

Chuck said, "Sure I can. Watch me. I just won't tell anybody he's dead."

A month later, the farmer met up with Chuck and asked,

"What happened with that dead donkey?"

Chuck said, "I raffled him off. I sold 500 tickets at two dollars apiece and made a profit of $898.00."

The farmer said, "Didn't anyone complain?""

Chuck said, "Just the guy who won. So I gave him his two dollars back."

A man walks into a bar and sits down at the counter.

The bartender comes up to him and says "What will it be?"

The man says "I'm having the worst day. I just found out my oldest son is gay. Give me a drink, in fact make it a double."

The bartender says "Oh that's terrible news."

He pours the drink and says "Here it is. If anybody deserves one you do."

The man drinks it and leaves.

A week later the man comes back into the bar sits down at the counter.

When the bartender comes up to him the man says, "I just found out my youngest son is gay. Give me a drink, in fact make it a double, no, make it a triple."

The bartender pours the drink and says "Here you go. This one's on the house."

The man drinks it and leaves.

A week later the same man comes back into the bar sits down at the counter.

The bartender recognizes the man and says, "Don't tell me... Isn't there anybody in your house that likes women?"

The man glumly replies, "Yeah, my wife!"

A man was depressed so he called the Depression Hotline.

He got a call center in Pakistan.

When he told them he was suicidal, they got all excited and asked if he knew how to drive a truck.

A boy went up to his father and asked him: "Dad, where did my intelligence come from?"

The father replied. "You must have got it from your mother, cause I still have mine."

A jumper cable works into a bar.

The bartender says, "Don't start anything."

An 18 year old girl tells her Mom that she has missed her period for 2 months. Very worried, the mother goes to the drugstore and buys a pregnancy kit. The test result shows that the girl is pregnant.

Shouting, cursing, crying, the mother says, "Who was the pig that did this to you? I want to know!"

The girl picks up the phone and makes a call. Half an hour later, a Ferrari stops in front of their house. A mature and distinguished man with grey hair and impeccably dressed in an Armani suit, steps out of a Ferrari and enters the house.

He sits in the living room with the father, mother, and the girl and tells them: "Good morning. Your daughter has informed me of the problem. I can't marry her because of my personal family situation but I'll take charge. I will pay all costs and provide for your daughter for the rest of her life. Additionally, if a girl is born, I will bequeath a Ferrari,

2 retail stores, a townhouse, a beach-front villa, and a $2,000,000 bank account. If a boy is born, my legacy will be a couple of factories and a $4,000,000 bank account.

If twins, they will receive a factory and $2,000,000 each. However, if there is a miscarriage, what do you suggest I do?"

At this point, the father, who had remained silent, places a hand firmly on the man's shoulder and tells him, "You're gonna try again."

Harry went to the doctor's office to get a double dose of Viagra.

The doctor told him that he couldn't allow him a double dose.

"Why not?", asked Harry.

"Because it's not safe," replied the doctor.

"But I need it really bad,' said Harry.

"Well, why do you need it so badly?" asked the doctor.

Harry said, "My girlfriend is coming into town on Friday; my ex-wife will be here on Saturday; and my wife is coming home on Sunday. Can't you see? I must have a double dose."

The doctor finally relented saying, "Okay, I'll give it to you, but you have to come in on Monday morning so that I can check you to see if there are any side effects."

On Monday, Harry dragged himself in; his right arm was in a sling.

The doctor asked, "What happened to you?"

Harry replied, "Nobody showed up."

A piano player, know for playing songs with off-color lyrics was playing in a lounge when he took a break to use the bathroom.

Upon his return to the piano, a patron walked up to him and said, "Do you know your zipper is open?"

The piano player replied, "Know it? I wrote it!"

One night, as a couple lays down for bed, the husband starts rubbing his wife's arm.

The wife turns over and says, "I'm sorry honey, I've got a gynecologist appointment tomorrow and I want to stay fresh."

The husband, rejected, turns over.

A few minutes later, he rolls back over and taps his wife again.

"Do you have a dentist appointment tomorrow too?"

A little boy is saying his prayers before bed.

He goes on with, "God bless Mommy, God bless Daddy, God bless Grandma. Good-bye Grandma."

The boy's father, hearing the boy's prayers, thinks it is strange, but doesn't say anything.

The next day the boy's grandmother dies. The father thinks this is just a coincidence.

The next night, the father listens while his son says his prayers before bed.

The boy goes on with, "God bless Mommy, God bless Daddy, God bless Grandpa. Good-bye Grandpa."

This worries the boy's father.

The next day the boy's grandfather dies. The father isn't sure what to think.

The next night, the father listens intently while his son says his prayers before bed.

The boy goes on with, "God bless Mommy, God bless Daddy. Good-bye Daddy."

This frightens the father. The next day he takes every precaution he can think of.

He doesn't use any electrical appliances, for fear of being electrocuted.

He walks to walk instead of driving, for fear of a car accident.

He doesn't eat anything, for fear of choking.

He does everything he can think of to ensure he remains safe.

Coming home exhausted, he proclaims to his wife, "You can't believe the day I had!"

His wife blurts out, "The day you had? The mailman dropped dead on the front porch."

Two men and a lady were stranded on a desert island. After a short time, the lady dies.

After a short time later, they felt so guilty about what they were doing, they buried her. A little while later, they felt so guilty about what they were doing, they un-buried her.

A man walks into a pharmacy and wanders up & down the aisles.
The sales girl notices him and asks him if she can help him.
He answers that he is looking for a box of tampons for his wife.
She directs him down the correct aisle.
A few minutes later, he puts a huge bag of cotton balls and a ball of string on the counter.
She says, confused, "Sir, I thought you were looking for some tampons for your wife?"
He answers, "You see, it's like this, yesterday, I sent my wife to the store to get me a carton of cigarettes, and she came back with a tin of tobacco and some rolling papers; cause it's sooo much cheaper. So, I figure if I have to roll my own .... So does she."

A man worked for a number of years in a pickle factory when he came home one day to confess to his wife that he had a terrible compulsion.
He had an urge to stick his penis into the pickle slicer.
His wife suggested that he should see a sex therapist to talk about it, but he said he would be too embarrassed. He vowed to overcome his compulsion on his own.
One day a few weeks later, Pete came home and his wife could see at once that something was seriously wrong.
"What's wrong?" she asked.
"Do you remember that I told you how I had this tremendous urge to put my penis into the pickle slicer?"
"Oh, you didn't?" she exclaimed.
"Yes, I did." he replied.
"My God, what happened?"
"I got fired."
"No. I mean, what happened with the pickle slicer?"
"Oh...she got fired too."

A man leaves for work, gets a block away and realizes he forgot his briefcase.
He heads back to the house and as he enters the phone rings.
He picks it and then yells, "How the hell should I know, call the Coast Guard!" and slams down the receiver.
His wife asks him, "Who was that, dear?"
The man states, "Just some joker wanting to know if the coast was clear"

While shopping for vacation clothes, a husband and wife passed a display of bathing suits. It had been at least ten years and twenty pounds since she had even considered buying a bathing suit, so she sought her husband's advice.
"What do you think?" she asked. "Should I get a bikini or an all-in-one?"
"Better get a bikini," he replied. "You'd never get it all in one."

Two men are in a bar getting drunk. Suddenly one of them throws up all over himself.
He says "Oh, no. Now my wife will kill me."
His friend says "Don't worry. Just tuck a twenty dollar bill in your breast pocket and tell your wife that someone threw up on you and gave you twenty dollars for the dry cleaning bill."
So they stay for another couple of hours and get even drunker.
Eventually he reels home and his wife starts to give him a bad time.
"You reek of alcohol and you've thrown up all over yourself, my God you're disgusting"
Speaking very carefully so as not to slur, he says, "Wait. It's not what you think. I only had one drink, but this man was sick on me. He'd obviously had one too many, or else he just couldn't hold his liquor. He was very sorry and he gave me twenty dollars for the cleaning bill. Look in my breast pocket."
She looks in his breast pocket and says, "But this is forty dollars."
"Ah, yes." says the man. "He pee'd in my trousers too."

Two men were stranded on a life raft in the middle of the ocean.
A little while later, they came across a peculiar looking bottle.
The first guy started to rub the bottle when a genie suddenly appeared and said he would grant him one wish.
The man though a second, then said, "I wish the ocean was all of my favorite beer."
Poof! The ocean is instantly changed to beer.
The second man says, "Great, now we have to pee in the boat!"

A woman was helping her husband set up his new computer, she told him he would now need to enter a password. Something he would remember and use to log-on.
Her husband figured he would be both clever and funny with his log-on id.
So, when the computer asked him to enter his password, he made it plainly obvious to his wife that he was keying in: P.... E... N... I... S...
His wife fell out of her chair laughing when the computer replied
PASSWORD INVALID.....NOT LONG ENOUGH

A man was sitting on the edge of the bed, observing his wife, looking at herself in the mirror. Since her birthday was not far off he asked what she'd like to have Birthday.

"I'd like to be six again", she replied, still looking in the mirror.

On the morning of her Birthday, he arose early, made her a nice big bowl of Lucky Charms, and then took her to Six Flags theme park. What a day!

He put her on every ride in the park; the Death Slide, the Wall of Fear, the Screaming Monster Roller Coaster, everything there was. Five hours later they staggered out of the theme park. Her head was reeling and her stomach felt upside down. He then took her to a McDonald's where he ordered her a Happy Meal with extra fries and a chocolate shake.

Then it was off to a movie, popcorn, a soda pop, and her favorite candy, M&M's.

What a fabulous adventure! Finally she wobbled home with her husband and collapsed into bed exhausted.

He leaned over his wife with a big smile and lovingly asked, "Well dear, what was it like being six again?"

Her eyes slowly opened and her expression suddenly changed. "I meant my dress size, you dumb ass!"

A drunk walks out of a bar with a key in his hand and he is stumbling back and forth.

A cop on the beat sees him and approaches, "Can I help you Sir?"

"Yessh! Ssssomebody ssstole my carrr", the man slurs.

The cop asks, "Where was your car the last time you saw it?"

"It wasss on the end of thisshh key", the man drunkenly replies.

About that time the cop looks down and sees the man's wiener hanging out of his fly for all of the world to see.

He asks the man, "Sir, are you aware that you are exposing yourself?"

Momentarily confused, the drunk looks down at his crotch and without missing a beat, blurts out...."Holy shit! My girlfriend's gone, too!!"

A guy walks into the bedroom carrying a sheep in his arms and says," Honey, this is the cow I make love to when you have a headache."

The wife, lying in bed, reading a book, looks up, shakes her head in disgust and says," If you weren't such an jack ass, you'd know that's a sheep, not a cow!"

The guy replies, "If you weren't such a presumptive bitch, you'd realize I was talking to the sheep!"

A man and his ever nagging wife went on vacation to Jerusalem. While there, the wife passed away.

The local undertaker told the husband, "You can have her shipped home for $5000 or you can bury her here in the holy land for $150."

The man thought about it and told him he would just have her shipped home.

The undertaker asked, "Why would you spend $5000 to ship your wife home, when it would be wonderful to be buried here and you would only spend $150?"

The man replied, "Long ago a man died here, was buried here, and three days later he rose from the dead. I just can't take that chance."

A man is stranded on a desert island. He's been there for years. One day, he sees a speck on the horizon. It gets larger and larger and a person in a black wet suit swims to shore.

Pulling off the scuba tank and face mask, he notices its a beautiful blonde woman.

She walks up to him and ask, "How long have you been stranded on this island?"

He replies, "I've been on this island for 7 years."

She asks him, "How long has it been since you had a good smoke?"

He replies, "Seven years."

She then unzips a waterproof pocket from her wetsuit and produces a fresh cigar and a lighter and gives it to him.

He takes the cigar, lights it and says, "I can't believe how much I missed these. It's great."

She then asks him, "How long has it been since you had a drink of whiskey?"

He replies, "Also seven years."

She unzips a different pocket, produces a flask and hands it to him.

He takes a sip and proclaims, "Oh, how I've missed the taste of this. It is truly fantastic."

At this point, the beautiful blond starts to slowly unzip her wetsuit down the middle.

She turns to him and asks, "How long has it been since you played around?"

With tears in his eyes he sobs, "Don't tell me you have a set of golf clubs in there too."

A husband and wife went for counseling after 25 years of marriage.

When asked what the problem was, the wife went into a passionate, painful tirade listing every problem they had ever had in the 25 years they had been married.

She went on and on and on: neglect, lack of intimacy, emptiness, loneliness, feeling unloved and unlovable, an entire laundry list of unmet needs she had endured over the course of their marriage.

Finally, after allowing this to go on for a sufficient length of time, the therapist got up, walked around the desk and after asking her to stand, embraced her, unbuttoned her blouse and bra, put his hands on her breasts and massaged them thoroughly, while kissing her passionately as her husband watched with a raised eyebrow!

She shut up, buttoned up her blouse, and quietly sat down while basking in the glow of being highly aroused.

The therapist turned to the husband and said, "This is what your wife needs at least three times a week.. Can you do this?"

He thought for a moment and replied, "Well, I can drop her off here on Mondays and Wednesdays, but on Fridays, I play golf."

A marine sergeant noticed a new recruit and ordered at him, "Get over her right now! What's your name soldier?"

The soldier replied, "It's John, sir."

The marine barked again, "I don't call anyone by their first name. It breeds familiarity which will lead to a breakdown in authority and respect. I refer to all my men by their last name, and you are to refer to me as Sergeant! Do I make myself clear?"

The soldier replied, "Yes sir, Sergeant."

The sergeant then stated, "Now that that's straight, what is your name?"

The soldier replied, "Darling... My name is John Darling."

The sergeant then said, "Ok John, here is what I want you to do."

A woman tells her husband that she wants to have plastic surgery to enlarge her breasts.

Her husband tells her, "You don't need surgery to do that, I know a way to do that without any surgery."

The wife asks, "How do I do it without surgery?"

The husband answers, "Just rub toilet paper between them."

The wife responds, "How will that make my breast bigger?"

The husband replies, "I don't know but it worked on your butt."

Bill decided to go skiing with his buddy, Bob. So they loaded up Jack's minivan and headed north.

After driving for a few hours, they got caught in a terrible blizzard. So they stopped a nearby farm. An attractive lady answered the door, they asked her if they could spend the night.

"I realize its terrible weather out there and I have this huge house all to myself, but I'm recently widowed," she explained. "I'm afraid the neighbors will talk if I let you stay in my house."

"Don't worry," Bill said. "We'll be happy to sleep in the barn. And if the weather breaks, we'll be gone at first light."

The lady agreed, and the two men found their way to the barn and settled in for the night.

Come morning, the weather had cleared, and they got on their way. They enjoyed a great weekend of skiing. But about nine months later, Jack got an unexpected letter from an attorney. It took him a few minutes to figure it out, but he finally determined that it was from the attorney of that attractive widow at the farm, he had met on the ski weekend.

He dropped in on his friend Bob and asked, "Bob, do you remember that good-looking widow from the farm we stayed at on our ski holiday up north about 9 months ago?"

Bob replied, "Why yes, I do."

"Did you, err, happen to get up in the middle of the night, go up to the house and pay her a visit?", Bill asked.

"Well, um, yes!" Bob said, a little embarrassed about being found out, "I have to admit that I did."

"And did you happen to give her my name instead of telling her your name?"

Bob's face turned beet red and he said, "Yeah, look, I'm sorry, buddy. I'm afraid I did Why do you ask?"

"She just died and left me everything."

A man walks into a diner and orders a hamburger. When the food arrives, he takes a bite out of it and notices a hair in the burger. He begins yelling frantically.

When the waitress comes over, he states "Waitress, there's a hair in my burger and I demand to speak to the cook ."

The waitress takes him into the kitchen where the man sees the cook take a meat patty and flatten it under his arm pit.

The man responds, "That's the most disgusting thing I've ever seen!"

The waitress replies, "If you think that's disgusting, you should see him make donuts!"

A husband and wife were laying in bad while watching 'Who Wants To Be A Millionaire'.
The husband turns to her and says, "Do you want to have sex?"
"No," she answered.
He then said, "Is that your final answer?"
She didn't even look at him and, simply said, "Yes."
So he said, "Then I'd like to phone a friend."

A man goes into a bar and orders a drink. He drinks it down nice and slow. When he finishes, he peeks inside his shirt pocket and states, "Not yet." Then orders another drink. This happens drink after drink.
Finally the bartender's curiosity gets the better of him and he asks the man, "Why do you look inside your shirt pocket and say 'Not yet', when you finish a drink?"
The man replies, "I have a picture of my wife in my pocket. When she starts looking good, I know I've had enough and it's time to head home."

When their lawn mower broke and wouldn't run, the wife kept hinting to her husband that he should get it fixed. But, somehow he always had something else to take care of first: the truck, the car, e-mail, fishing, always something more important to him.
Finally she thought of a clever way to make her point.
When he arrived home one day, he found her seated in the tall grass, busily snipping away with a tiny pair of sewing scissors. He watched silently for a short time and then went into the house. When he came out again he handed her a toothbrush.
"When you finish cutting the grass," he said, "You might as well sweep the driveway.'"

A man tried to talk his wife into buying a case of beer for $14.95.
Instead, she bought a jar of cold cream for $7.95.
He told her the beer would make her look better at night than the cold cream.

Religious

There was an old priest who got sick of all the people in his parish who kept confessing to adultery.

One Sunday, he said, "If I hear one more person confess to adultery, I'll quit!" Everyone liked him, so they came up with a code word. Someone who had committed adultery would say instead that they had "fallen."

This seemed to satisfy the old priest and things went well until the priest passed away at a ripe, old age.

A few days after the new priest arrived, he visited the mayor of the town and seemed very concerned.

"Mayor, you have to do something about the sidewalks in town. When people come into the confessional, they keep telling me they've fallen."

The mayor started to laugh, realizing that no one had told the new priest about the code word. But, before he could explain, the priest shook an accusing finger at him and shouted, "I don't know what you're laughing about, because your wife has already fallen three times this week!"

One Sunday morning, a minister announced to his congregation: "My good people, I have here in my hands three sermons... a $100 sermon that lasts five minutes, a $50 sermon that lasts fifteen minutes, and a $10 sermon that lasts a full hour. Now, we'll take the collection and see which one I'll deliver."

A priest, a minister and a rabbi walk into a bar.
The bartender says, "What is this ... a joke?"

A man goes to the cemetery to put flowers on his parents grave when he notices a man nearby crying and saying "Why? Why? It's just not fair. Why did you have to die?"

The man goes about his business, but the man nearby keeps on wailing "It's just not fair. Why? Why did you have to die?"

Finally the man goes over to the crying man and says, "I couldn't help but overhear you. I am so sorry for you loss. Did you lose a child?"

The man sobs out, "No."

"A spouse?"

The man again sobs out, "No."

"If I may ask, who is all the crying for?"

The man replies thru his anguish," My wife's first husband. It's just not fair. Why? Why did he have to die."

St. Peter was guarding the Pearly Gates, waiting for new souls coming to heaven.

He saw Jesus walking by and caught his attention. "Jesus, could you mind the gate while I go do an errand?"

"Sure," replied Jesus. "What do I have to do?"

"Just find out about the people who arrive. Ask about their background, their family, and their lives. Then decide if they deserve entry into Heaven."

"Sounds easy enough. OK.", said Jesus.

So Jesus manned the gates for St. Peter. The first person to approach the gates was a wrinkled old man. Jesus summoned him to sit down and sat across from him. Jesus peered at the old man and asked, "What did you do for a living?"

The old man replied, "I was a carpenter."

Jesus remembered his own earthly existence and leaned forward. "Did you have any family?" he asked.

"Yes, I had a son, but I lost him."

Jesus leaned forward some more. "You lost your son? Can you tell me about him?"

"Well, he had holes in his hands and feet."

Jesus leaned forward even more and whispered, "Father?"

The old man leaned forward and whispered, "Pinocchio?"

A young minister is asked by a funeral director to hold a grave side service for a homeless man with no family or friends. The funeral was to be at a cemetery way out in the country. This was a new cemetery and this man was the first to be laid to rest there.

The minister was not familiar with the area and became lost. Being a typical man, of course, he did not ask for directions. He finally found the cemetery about an hour late. The back hoe was there and the crew was eating their lunch. The hearse was not around.

He apologized to the workers for being late, looked into the open grave, saw the vault lid already in place and told the workers that he would not keep them long .The workers, still eating their lunch, gathered around the opening.

The young minister was enthusiastic and poured out his heart and soul as he preached. The workers joined in with, "Praise the Lord," "Amen," and "Glory!"

When the service was over, he said a prayer and walked to his car. As he opened the door, he heard one of the workers say, "I never saw anything like that before and I've been putting in septic systems for twenty years."

Adam was hanging around the garden of Eden feeling very lonely.

So, God asked him, "What's wrong with you?"

Adam said he didn't have anyone to talk to.

God said that He was going to make Adam a companion and that it would be a woman.

He said, "This pretty lady will gather food for you, she will cook for you, and when you discover clothing, she will wash them for you.

She will always agree with every decision you make and she will not nag you, and will always be the first to admit she was wrong when you've had a disagreement. She will praise you! She will bear your children and never ask you to get up in the middle of the night to take care of them. She will NEVER have a headache and will freely give you love and passion whenever you need it."

Adam asked God, "What will a woman like this cost?"

"An arm and a leg," God replied.

Then Adam asked, "What can I get for a rib?"

A man dies and finds himself in Hell.

He is quite upset and depressed, until he meets the devil.

The devil tells him he shouldn't be so upset, it's not really that bad here.

The devil asks the man, "Did you like to smoke?"

The man replies, "I smoked some what on Earth."

The devil says that's good, because on Monday, all we do is smoke, we smoke cigarettes, then we smoke cigars, then we smoke pipes. We smoke and smoke and smoke until we get sick, then smoke some more. What difference does it matter. You are dead anyway!"

The devil then asks the man, "Did you like to drink?"

The man replies, "Yes, I did like to drink."

The devil says that's good, because on Tuesday, all we do is drink, we drink beer, then we drink whiskey, then we drink shots, then we drink tequila. We drink and drink and drink until we get sick, then drink some more. It doesn't matter. You're dead."

The devil then says to the man, "See it's not so bad. Do you like to gamble?"

The man excitedly replies "Yes, yes I do like to gamble."

The devil says that's good, because on Wednesday, all we do is gamble, we play poker, we play slots, we play blackjack, we play roulette, We gamble all day and then gamble some more. What difference does it matter. You're dead anyway!"

The man thinks maybe it isn't so bad after all.

The devil then asks the man, "Are you gay?"

The man says, "No, I'm not!"

The devil says, "Oh…, then you are not going to like Fridays!"

One morning a man came into the church on crutches. He stopped in front of the holy water, put some on both legs, and then threw away his crutches.

An altar boy witnessed the scene and then ran into the rectory to tell the priest what he'd just seen.

"Son, you've just witnessed a miracle!" the priest said. "Tell me, where is this man now?"

"Flat on his butt over by the holy water!" the boy informed him.

A cabbie picks up a nun and when she settles in, the cab driver won't stop staring at her.

She asks him why he is staring.

He replies: "I have a question to ask you, but I don't want to offend you."

She answers, "My son, you cannot offend me. When you're as old as I am and have been a nun as long as I have, you get a chance to see and hear just about everything. I'm sure that there's nothing you could say or ask that I would find offensive."

"Well, I've always had a fantasy to have a nun kiss me."

She responds, "Well, let's see what we can do about that. But first, you have to be single and you must be Catholic."

The cab driver is very excited and says, "Yes, I'm single and Catholic!"

"OK" the nun says. "Pull into the next alley, maybe we will see what we can do."

The nun fulfills his fantasy with a kiss that would make a hooker blush. But when they get back on the road, the cab driver starts crying.

"My dear child," said the nun, why are you crying?"

"Forgive me, but I've sinned. I lied. I must confess, I'm married and I'm Jewish."

The nun says, "That's OK, my name is Kevin and I'm going to a Halloween party."

A preacher was about to start his sermon, when he announced," Whoever donates $1000 can pick the next 3 hymns."

An old lady in the back stood up and said she would do it.

The minister said, "Ok, you can pick the hymns."

She looked over the congregation and said. "I'll pick him and him and him."

The 7 Dwarfs go to the Vatican and, because they are the 7 Dwarfs, they are immediately ushered in to see the Pope. Grumpy leads the pack.

"Grumpy, my son," says the Pope, "What can I do for you?"'

Grumpy asks, "Excuse me your Excellency, but are there any dwarf nuns in Rome?"

The Pope wrinkles his brow at the odd question, thinks for a moment and then answers, "No, Grumpy, there are no dwarf nuns in Rome."

In the background, a few of the dwarfs start giggling.

Grumpy turns around and glares, silencing them.

Grumpy turns back, "Your Worship, are there any dwarf nuns in all of Europe?"

The Pope, puzzled now, again thinks for a moment and then answers, "'No, Grumpy, there are no dwarf nuns in all of Europe."

This time, all of the other dwarfs burst into laughter.

Once again, Grumpy turns around and silences them with an angry glare.

Grumpy turns back and says, "Mr. Pope! Are there ANY dwarf nuns anywhere in the world?"

The Pope, really confused by the questions says, "I'm sorry, my son, there are no dwarf nuns anywhere in the world."

The other dwarfs collapse into a heap, rolling and laughing, pounding the floor, tears rolling down their cheeks, as they begin chanting......

"Grumpy screwed a penguin!"

"Grumpy screwed a penguin!"

A pastor who was badly overworked went to the local medical center and was able to have a clone made. The clone was like the pastor in every respect-- except that the clone used extraordinarily foul language. The cloned pastor was exceptionally gifted in many other areas of pastoral work, but finally the complaints about the dirty language were too much. The pastor was not too sure how to get rid of the clone so that it wouldn't look like murder. The best thing, he decided, was to make the clone's death look like an accident. So the pastor lured the clone onto a bridge in the middle of the night and pushed the clone off the bridge. Unfortunately there was a police officer who happened by at that very moment and arrested the pastor for making an obscene clone fall.

While walking down the street one day, a US senator is tragically hit by a truck and dies.

His soul arrives in heaven and is met by St. Peter at the entrance.

"Welcome to heaven," says St. Peter. "Before you settle in, it seems there is a problem. We seldom see a high official around these parts. So we're not sure what to do with you."

"No problem, just let me in," says the senator.

"Well, I'd like to, but I have orders from higher up. What we'll do is have you spend one day in hell and one in heaven. Then you can choose where to spend eternity."

"Really, I've made up my mind. I want to be in heaven," says the senator.

"I'm sorry, but we have our rules."

And with that, St. Peter escorts him to the elevator and he goes down, down, down to hell. The doors open and he finds himself in the middle of a green golf course. In the distance is a clubhouse and standing in front of it are all his friends and other politicians
who had worked with him.

Everyone is very happy and in evening dress. They run to greet him, shake his hand, and reminisce about the good times they had while getting rich at the expense of the people.

They play a friendly game of golf and then dine on lobster, caviar
and champagne.

Also present is the devil, who really is a very friendly guy who has a good time dancing and telling jokes. They are having such a good time that before he realizes it, it is time to go. Everyone gives him a hearty farewell and waves while the elevator rises...

The elevator goes up, up, up and the door reopens on heaven where St. Peter is waiting.

"Now it's time to visit heaven," says St. Peter.

So, 24 hours pass with the senator joining a group of contented souls moving from cloud to cloud, playing the harp and singing. They have a good time and, before he realizes it, the 24 hours have gone by and St. Peter returns.

"Well, then, you've spent a day in hell and another in heaven. Now choose your eternity."

The senator reflects for a minute, then he answers: "Well, I would never have said it before, I mean heaven has been delightful, but I think I would be better off in hell."

So St. Peter escorts him to the elevator and he goes down, down, down to hell. Now the doors of the elevator open and he's in the middle of a barren land covered with waste and garbage. He sees all his friends, dressed in rags, picking up the trash and putting it in black bags as more trash falls from above.

The devil comes over to him and puts his arm around his shoulder.

"I don't understand," stammers the senator. "Yesterday I was here and there was a golf course and clubhouse, and we ate lobster and caviar, drank champagne, and danced and had a great time. Now there's just a wasteland full of garbage and my friends look
miserable. What happened?"

The devil looks at him, smiles and says, "Yesterday we were campaigning... Today you voted."

Three men die in a car accident Christmas Eve. They all find themselves at the pearly gates waiting to enter Heaven. On entering they must present something related to or associated with Christmas.

The first man searches his pockets and finds mistletoe, so he is allowed in.

The second man presents a candy cane, so he is also allowed in.

The third man pulls out a pair of stockings.

Confused at this last gesture, St. Peter asks, "How do these represent Christmas?"

"They're Carol's", he states.

A hippie boards a bus and spies a pretty young Nun.

He sits down next to her, and asks: "Can we have sex?"

"No," she replies, "I'm married to God."

She stands up and gets off at the next stop.

The bus driver turns to the hippie and says: "I know how you can have sex with her!"

"Yeah?" says the hippie.

"Yeah!" says the bus driver. "She goes to the cemetery every Tuesday night at midnight to pray, so all you have to do is dress up in a robe with a hood, put some of that luminous powder stuff in your beard, and pop up in the cemetery claiming to be God."

The next Tuesday night, the hippie arrives in the cemetery dressed as suggested. "I am God," he declares to the nun, keeping the hood low. "Have sex with me!"

The nun agrees without question, but begs him to restrict himself to anal sex, as she is desperate not to lose her virginity.

'God' agrees and promptly has his wicked way with her. As he finishes, he jumps up and throws back his hood with a flourish. "Ha-ha" he cries, "I'm the hippie from the bus!"

"Ha-ha" cries the nun tossing back her veil. "I'm the bus driver!"

While attending a Marriage Seminar dealing with communication, a couple listened to the pastor, "It is essential that husbands and wives know each other's likes and dislikes."

He addressed the man, "Can you name your wife's favorite flower?"

He leaned over, touched his wife's arm gently and whispered, "It's Pillsbury, isn't it?"

A lady owned a cockatoo that always asked, "Who is it?", whenever the door bell rang.

One day, a plumber arrived while the lady was out, and rang the bell.

The cockatoo asked "Who is it?"

The poor guy said, "It's the plumber",

But the bird just kept repeating 'Who is it!' Every time the old guy would say 'It's the plumber', until the frustrated plumber fell dead on our porch with a stroke.

When she came home, she saw the body and said, "Oh My God....Who is this?"

The bird shouted...."It's the plumber!"

A man went to the confessional. "Forgive me, Father, for I have sinned."

"What is your sin, my son?" the priest asked.

"Well," the man started, "I used some horrible language this week, and I feel terrible."

"When did you use this awful language?" asked the priest.

"I was golfing and hit an incredible drive that looked like it was going to go over 250 yards, but it struck a power line that was hanging over the fairway and fell straight down to the ground after going only about a hundred yards."

"Is that when you swore?"

"No, Father. After that, a squirrel ran out of the bushes and grabbed my ball in his mouth and began to run away."

"Is that when you swore?"

"Well, no. You see, as the squirrel was running, an eagle came down out of the sky, grabbed the squirrel in his talons, and flew away!"

"Is *that* when you swore?" asked the amazed priest.

"No, not yet. As the eagle carried the squirrel away in his claws, it flew toward the green. And as it passed over a bit of forest near the green, the squirrel dropped my ball."

"Did you swear then?"

"No, because as the ball felt it struck a tree, bounced through some bushes, careened off a big rock, and rolled through a sand trap onto the green and stopped within six inches of the hole."

The priest signed, "You missed the putt, didn't you?"

The graveside service just barely finished, when there was massive
clap of thunder, followed by a tremendous bolt of lightning, accompanied by
even more thunder rumbling in the distance.
The little old man looked at the pastor and calmly said, "Well, she's there."

A nun was walking home one evening when a man came up from behind and
whispered "Forgive me, but I've always fantasized about making love to a nun.
Are you willing?"
The nun nodded meekly.
The man walked her into the woods, pulled off her clothes and had his way
with her.
Feeling quite pleased, he asked her, "What are you going to tell Mother
Superior?"
The nun replied, "I'm going to tell the truth. A man grabbed, me pulled me into
the woods and had his way with me. Twice, if he's not too tired."

Two Nuns are riding their bicycles down the back streets of Rome.
One leans over to the other and says, "I've never come this way before."
The first Nun whispers, "It's the cobblestones."

A man calls his local church and asks to speak with the head pig at the trough.
The receptionist is quite offended at that remark and states, "That is not a very
polite thing to say. We refer to him as the Pastor."
The caller replies, "Well I was going to make a $10,000 donation to the church."
The receptionist replies, "I think Porky just walked in."

A drunk smelling like beer, sat down on a subway next to a priest. The man's
shirt was stained, his face was plastered with red lipstick, and a half-empty bottle
of gin was sticking out of his torn coat pocket. He opened his newspaper and
began reading.
After a few minutes, the man turned to the priest and asked, "Say Father, what
causes arthritis?"
The priest replies, "My son, its caused by loose living, being with cheap wicked
women, too much alcohol, contempt for your fellow man, sleeping around with
prostitutes and lack of bath."
The drunk mutter, "Well I'll be damned", then returned to his paper.
The priest, thinking about what he had said, nudged the man and apologized,
"I'm very sorry. I didn't mean to come on so strong. How long have you had
arthritis?"
The drunk answered, "I don't have it, Father. I was just reading here that the
Pope does."

Three men were sitting on a bench in heaven discussing how they died.
The first man said, "I died of cancer."
The second man said, "I died of a heart attack."
The third man said," I died of seenus."
The first two men said," Did you mean sinus?"
The third man said. "No, I mean seenus. I was out with my best friends wife and he seen us!"

Answering the phone, the priest was surprised to hear the caller was an IRS auditor.
"But we don't pay taxes" the priest said.
"This call isn't about you, father. It is about one of your parishioners, A Sam McGill.
He indicates he gave a donation of $15,000 to the church last year. Is this the truth?"
The priest smiled broadly and replied, "The check hasn't arrived yet, but I'm sure it will when I remind him of this call."

A cowboy appeared before St. Peter at the Pearly Gates.
"Have you ever done anything of particular merit?" St. Peter asked.
"Well, I can think of one thing", the cowboy offered, "On a trip out in South Dakota, I came across a gang of bikers, who were threatening a young woman. I directed them to leave her alone, but they wouldn't listen. SO I approached the largest and most heavily tattooed biker and smacked him in the face, kicked his bike over, ripped out his nose ring and threw it to the ground.
Then I yelled," Now back off right now!! Or I'll kick the living shit out of all of you!"
St. Peter was impressed, "Really, when did this happen?"
"Just a couple of minutes ago..."

Moe: "My wife got me to believe in religion."
Joe: "Really?"
Moe: "Yeah. Until I married her I didn't believe in Hell."

I used to be an Atheist, but there weren't enough holidays.

What happens if an Atheist lies under oath?

Q. How do you make holy water?
A. You boil the Hell out of it.

A bus on a busy street strikes a Catholic man.

He is lying near death on the sidewalk as a crowd gathers.

"A priest! Please, somebody get me a priest!" the man gasped.

Long seconds dragged on but no one stepped out of the crowd.

A policeman checked the crowd and finally yelled, "A PRIEST, PLEASE! Isn't there a priest in this crowd to give this man his last rites?"

Finally, out of the crowd stepped a little old Jewish man in his 80's.

"Officer," said the man, "I'm not a priest. I'm not even a Christian. But for 50 years now, I'm living behind the Catholic Church on Second Avenue, and every night I am overhearing their services ... I can recall a lot of it, and maybe I can be of some comfort to this poor man."

The policeman agreed, and cleared the crowd so the man could get through to where the injured man lay.

The old Jewish man knelt down, leaned over the man and said in a solemn voice, "B-4... I-19... N-38... G-54.... O-72"

One Sunday morning, a pastor asked if anyone in the congregation would like to express praise for an answered prayer.

A lady stood up and walked to the podium and said, "I have praise. Two months ago, my husband Tom had a terrible bicycle wreck and his scrotum was completely crushed. The pain was excruciating and the doctors didn't know if they could help him."

A muffled gasp was heard from all the men in the congregation as they imagined the pain that poor Tom must have experienced.

"Tom was unable to hold me or the children, "she went on, "and every move caused him terrible pain. We prayed as the doctors performed a delicate operation, and it turned out they were able to piece together the crushed remains of his scrotum, wrap wire around it and hold it in place."

Again all the men were unnerved and squirmed uncomfortably as they imagined the horrible surgery performed on Tom.

"Now," she announced, "I want to thank the good Lord that my Tom is out of the hospital and the doctors say that with time his scrotum should recover completely."

All the men let out a collected sigh of relief, as the woman sat down.

The pastor rose and asked if anyone else had anything to say.

A man stood up, walked slowly to the podium and said, "I'm Tom, and I just want to tell my wife that the word is sternum. My *sternum* was completely crushed."

The church organist was in her eighties and had never been married.
She was admired for her sweetness and kindness to all.
One afternoon the pastor came to call on her and she showed him into her
quaint sitting room. She invited him to have a seat while she prepared tea.
As he sat facing her old Hammond organ, the young minister noticed a cute
glass bowl sitting on top of it. The bowl was filled with water, and in the water
floated, of all things, a condom! When she returned with tea, they began to chat.
The pastor tried to stifle his curiosity about the bowl of water and its strange
floater, but soon it got the better of him and he could no longer resist.
Pointing to the bowl, he asked her, "I wonder if you would tell me about this?"
"Oh, yes," she replied, "Isn't it wonderful? I was walking through the park a few
months ago and I found this little package on the ground. The directions said to
place it on the organ, keep it wet and that it would prevent the spread of
disease. Do you know I haven't had the flu all winter?"

One day when the Pope was on tour, he decided he wanted to drive.
At first his driver wouldn't allow it, but the Pope convinces him it will be Ok.
The driver finally heads to the back seat, while the Pope gets behind the wheel
and starts to drive .
Suddenly the Pope floors it, pushing the petal to the metal. He keeps this up
getting the limo over 100 mph.
Eventually he hears sirens behind him and sees a police cruiser in the rear
window.
The Pope pulls over and rolls down the window as the officer approaches.
The officer takes one look at him and goes back to the cruiser and gets on the
radio.
He tells the chief that he stopped a limo doing over 100 mph.
"So arrest him", states the chief.
The officer replies, "I don't think we should do that. He's really important."
The chief says, "All the more reason".
The officer responds, "No he's **really** important"
The chief asks, "Who do you have there? The Mayor?"
The officer responds, "Bigger."
The chief asks, "A Senator?"
The officer responds , "Bigger."
The chief asks, "The Governor?"
The officer responds, "Bigger."
The chief asks, "Who is it then?"
The officer replies, "I think its God."
The chief is curious now and asks, "Why do you think its God?"
The officer states, "Because his chauffeur is the Pope!"

A man suffered a heart attack and had to have open heart surgery. He awakened from surgery to find himself in the care of a nun at a Catholic Hospital.

As he was waking up, a nun came over and started asking him questions on how he was going to pay for his care and treatment.

He wearily replied, "I have no health insurance."

The nun asked him if he had any money in the bank.

He again wearily replied, "I have no money."

The nun asked him if he had any relatives who could help.

He replied, "I only have a spinster sister who is a nun."

The nun, very annoyed, said, "Nuns are not spinsters. We are married to God!".

He replied, "Great. My brother-in-law will handle the bill."

An old country preacher had a teenage son and it was getting time for the boy to be thinking about a profession. One day while the boy was at school, his father decided to try something. He went into the boys room and placed the following four items on the dresser.

1. A Bible
2. A silver dollar
3. A bottle of whisky
4. A playboy magazine

He thought that he would hide in his son's room and see which item his son would pick-up when he came home from school. The preacher figured if its the Bible, then his son is going to be a preacher like him, if it's the silver dollar, then he would be a businessman.

But if his son picks up the bottle of whisky, then he is going to a drunken bum and worst of all if he picked up the playboy magazine, he would be a skirt chasing womanizer.

Soon he heard his son footsteps coming up to the house. The preacher ran and hid in his son's room, behind the door. The son entered his room, put his schoolbooks on the bed, saw the items on the dresser and went over to them. After looking at all 4 items, he picked up the Bible and placed it under his arm, picked up the silver dollar and dropped it in his pocket. He opened the bottle and took a big drink while turning the magazine and admiring this months centerfold.

The preacher saw all of this and thought, "Oh no. He's going to run for congress!"

A Sunday school nun was asking her class what they wanted to be when they grow up. One little girl said, "When I grow up, I want to be a prostitute".

The nun was horrified, "WHAT? What did you just say?"

The girl repeated, "When I grow up, I want to be a prostitute".

The nun replies, "Oh Thank Heavens. For a second there, I thought you said 'Protestant'."

Four Catholic men and one Catholic woman were having coffee.

The first Catholic man tells his friends, "My son is a priest, when he walks into a room, everyone calls him 'Father'."

The second Catholic man jumps in with, "My son is a Bishop. When he walks into a room people call him 'Your Grace'."

The third Catholic man says, "My son is a Cardinal. When he enters a room everyone says 'Your Eminence'."

The fourth Catholic man then says, "My son is the Pope. When he walks into a room people call him 'Your Holiness'."

Since the lone Catholic woman was sipping her coffee in silence, the four men give her a subtle, "Well....?"

She proudly replies, "I have a daughter, slim, tall, 38D breast, 24 inch waist and 34 inch hips. When she walks into a room, people say, "Oh My God!"

A Baptist lived among a group of Catholics and every Friday while the Catholics were eating fish, the Baptist would be on his patio grilling a steak. The Catholics decided they were going to get the Baptist to convert to Catholicism. After convincing him to convert, he received a baptism from the local priest .

As the priest was sprinkling water on the man, the priest said to him, "You were born a Baptist, you were raised a Baptist, but today you are a Catholic."

The next Friday, while the Catholics were eating fish, they smelled a steak grilling. It was coming from the former Baptists patio. The went over to his house to confront him.

They saw him sprinkling water on the steak saying, " You were born a cow, you were raised a cow, but today you are a fish."

Ethnic

Q. What do you call a Mexican baptism?
A. A bean dip.

Q. What did the Mexican do with his first 50-cent piece?
A. He married her.

Q. What did Jesus say to the Mexicans?
A. Don't do anything 'till I get back.

Q. Why don't they have the Olympics in Mexico?
A. Because anyone who can run, jump, or swim, is already here.

Two Mexican detectives were investigating the murder of Juan Gonzalez.
"How was he killed?" asked one detective.
"With a golf gun," the other detective replied.
"A golf gun! What is a golf gun?", the first detective asked.
"I don't know. But it sure made a hole in Juan."

Q. What do you get if a Black man marries a Mexican woman?
A. Children too stupid to steal.

Q. What are the 3 things you can't give a Black man?
A. A fat lip, a black eye and a tan.

Q. What do you call 100 Blacks buried up to their heads?
A. Afro turf.

Q. Why do black people smell so bad?
A. So blind people can hate them too.

Q. What is a 7 course meal to an Irishman?
A. A six-pack and a potato.

An Irish woman is making dinner, when a police officer shows up.
"I'm sorry ma'am, I got some bad news to tell you", he says.
"There was an accident at the Guinness Brewery. You husband Shamus is dead.
He fell into a vat of Guinness Stout and drowned."
"O, my dear! You must tell me, did he at least go quickly?" she replied.
"No. In fact he got out twice to pee."

Q. How many Pollack's does it take to change a light bulb?
A. 1001, 1 to hold the light bulb and 1000 to turn the house.

Q. How do you know the Polish mafia is in town!
A. They find two guys in an alley with their heads tied together, shot in the hands!

Q. What is the hardest thing a Polish man gives his wife on their honeymoon?
A. His name.

A gentleman had been trying for years to meet the Pope. Finally, his wish was granted. When the gentleman approached the Pope he said, "Your Eminence, I am so happy to be given this chance to speak with you and I would like to tell you a joke before I start."
The Pope replied, "Of course my son. Go ahead and tell your joke."
The gentleman continued, "There were these two Pollack's and..."
The Pope interrupted, "My son, do you realize that I am Polish?"
"I'm sorry, your Eminence, I'll speak slower."

A Polish man was suffering from constipation, so his doctor prescribed suppositories.
A week later the Pole complains to the doctor that they didn't produce the desired results.
"Have you been taking them regularly?" the doctor asked.
"What do you think I've been doing," the Pole said, "Shoving them up my ass?"

Q. How do you drive a Jew crazy?
A. Put him in a round room, and tell him there is a penny in the corner.

Q. How does a Jew play hide and seek?
A. He covers his eyes and counts...97, 98, 99, a dollar, ready or not here I come.

Q. What do you get when you cut a bra in half?
A. Two Yarmulkes with chin straps.

Q. Why do Jews have big noses?
A. Because the air is free.

A bus stops at a bus stop, and two Italian men get on.
They sit down and engage in an animated conversation.
The lady sitting next to them ignores them at first, but her attention is
galvanized when she hears one of them say the following: "Emma come
first. Den I come. Den two asses come together. I come once-a-more! Two
asses, they come together again. I come again and pee twice. Then I come one
lasta time."
The lady can't take this any more, "You foul-mouthed sex obsessed pig." She
retorted indignantly. "In this country, we don't speak aloud in public places
about our sex lives."
"Hey, coola down lady," said the Italian. "Who a talkin' about a sex? I'm a just a
tellin my friend a how to spell ' Mississippi. "

Two old Italians guys, one 80 and one 87, were sitting on their usual park bench
one morning. The 87 year old had just finished his morning jog and wasn't even
short of breath. The 80 year old was amazed at his friend's stamina and asked
him what he did to have so much energy.
The 87 year old said, "Well, I eat Italian bread every day. It keeps your energy
level high and you'll have great stamina with the ladies."
So, on the way home, the 80 year old stops at the bakery. As he was looking
around, the lady asked if he needed any help.
He said, "Do you have any Italian bread "
She said, "Yes, there's a whole shelf of it. Would you like some?"
He said, "Yes, I want 5 loaves."
She said, "My goodness, 5 loaves .... By the time you get to the 5th loaf, it'll be
hard."
He replied, "I can't believe it, everybody knows about this but me."

Q. Why do Italian men have mustaches?
A. So they can look like their mothers.

Q. Why does the 2nd Italian navy have glass bottom boats?
A. So they can see the1st Italian navy.

Italian position, man on top, women in kitchen.

An old Italian lived alone in New Jersey. He wanted to plant his annual tomato garden, but it was very difficult work as the ground was hard. His only son, who used to help him, was in prison.

The old man wrote a letter to his son and described his predicament:

"Dear son:

I am feeling pretty sad, because it looks like I won't be able to plant my tomato garden this year. I'm just getting too old to be digging up a garden plot. I know if you were here my troubles would be over. I know you would be happy to dig the plot for me, like before

Love, Papa"

A few days later he received a letter from his son,

"Dear Pop:

Don't dig up that garden. That's where the bodies are buried."

At 4 a.m. the next morning, FBI agents and local police arrived and dug up the entire area without finding any bodies. They apologized to the old man and left. That same day the old man received another letter from his son.

"Dear Pop:

Go ahead and plant the tomatoes now. That is the best I could do under the circumstances."

A Scotsman is about to be married. He is down at the local tavern having a beer when he decides to ask the bartender for some advice.

"McGregor, I am about to be marrying my sweet lass. How can I tell if she's still a virgin", he asks.

"'Tis a good question, me lad, 'Tis a very good question. Have her put her hand under your kilt and ask her what she feels. If she says she feels a cock, then she's been around a bit, and not a virgin." says the bartender.

"'Tis good advice. 'Tis very good advice indeed." he says.

The next day he is out with his bride to be, and tells her," Aye, me lassie, put you hand under my kilt, and tell me what you feel."

She does and says," 'Tis a worm. 'Tis a worm indeed!"

The Scotsman is happy with her answer and soon they get married.

After the wedding, her asks her again, "Aye, me sweet lassie, put you hand under my kilt, and tell me what you feel."

She does and says," 'Tis a worm. 'Tis a worm indeed!"

He corrects her and proudly states, "No, No. 'Tis a cock, Not repeat that. 'Tis a cock"

She replies," No. 'Tis a worm. Now McGregor, he has a cock, but you have a worm!"

A Scotsman walks out of a bar...

A young Chinese couple gets married. She is a virgin. On their wedding night, she cowers naked under the sheets as her husband undresses in the darkness. He climbs into the bed next to her and tries to be reassuring.
He whispers," I know you are frightened. I'll promise I will do anything you want."
A thoughtful silence follows and he waits patiently for her request.
She eventually whispers back," I want to try something I have heard about from other girls… Number 69." More thoughtful silence, this time from him.
Eventually, in a puzzled tone, he asks her," You want garlic chicken with snow peas?"

Q. What do you call a fat 'Chink'?
A. A chunk.

A Canadian lady was walking down the street, when she meets up with a priest. The Father said, "Hello there. Didn't I marry you and your husband 2 years ago?"
She says, "Why yes, yes you did, Father"
The Father asks, "Are there any little ones yet?"
She replies, "No, not yet, Father."
The Father says, "Well I'm going to Rome next week and I'll light a candle for you and your husband" Then they parted ways. Some years later they ran into each other.
The Father recognizes her and asks, "Hello. How are you? Are there any little ones yet?" The lady replies, "I am fine, Father. And yes Father, Three sets of twins and a single"
The Father says, "That's wonderful! How is your husband doing?"
The lady replies, "He's gone to Rome."
The Father asks, "Rome? What takes your husband to Rome?"
The lady replies, "To blow out your freakin candle."

A Canadian is having breakfast, in Paris, one morning (coffee, croissants, bread, butter and jam) when a Frenchman, chewing bubble-gum, sits down next to him. The Canadian ignores the Frenchman who, nevertheless, starts a conversation.

Frenchman: "You Canadian folk eat the whole bread?"

Canadian (in a bad mood): "Of course."

Frenchman: (after blowing a huge bubble) "We don't. In France, we only eat what's inside. The crusts we collect, make them into croissants and sell them to the Canadians."

The Canadian listens in silence.

The Frenchman persists: "Do you eat jelly with the bread?"

Canadian: "Of Course."

Frenchman: (cracking his bubble-gum between his teeth and chuckling). "We don't. In France we eat fresh fruit for breakfast, then we put all the peels, seeds, and leftovers in containers, transform them into jam, and sell the jam to the Canadians."

After a moment of silence, The Canadian then asks: "Do you have sex in France?"

Frenchman: "Why of course we do", he says with a big smirk.

Canadian: "And what do you do with the condoms once you've used them?"

Frenchman: "We throw them away, of course."

Canadian: "We don't. In Canada, we put them in a container, recycle them, melt them down into bubble-gum, and sell them to French."

Q. What's the difference between a Canadian and a canoe?
A. A canoe tips.

Q. What happens if an Eskimo sits on ice to long?
A. He gets a Polaroid.

A young American Indian brave goes up to the elder of the tribe and says, "Great leader, is it true, that you when the babies are born, you decide their names by what you see around you?"
The elder American Indian states, "That is true. If I see a gentle stream running, I might name the baby 'running stream', or if I see a shining full moon, I might name the little one 'Moonbeam'." Then the elder Indian says, "Why do you ask Twodogsfucking?"

A man asked an American Indian what was his wife's name.
The American Indian replied "She called Five Horse."
The man said, "That's an unusual name for your wife. What does it mean?"
The old Indian replied, "It old Indian name. It mean NAG, NAG, NAG, NAG, NAG."

One day God went to the Arabs and said,
"I have some Commandments for you that will make your lives better."
The Arabs asked, "What are Commandments?"
And the Lord said, "They are rules for living. "
"Can you give us an example?", they asked.
"Thou shall not kill."
"Not kill?   We're not interested", they replied.
So He went to the blacks and said, "I have some Commandments."
The blacks wanted an example, and the Lord said, "Honor thy Father and Mother."
"Father? We don't know who our fathers are. We're not interested", they replied
Then He went to the Mexicans and said, "I have some Commandments."
The Mexicans also wanted an example, and the Lord said, "Thou shall not steal."
"Not steal? We're not interested", they replied
Then He went to the French and said, "I have some commandments."
The French too wanted an example and the Lord said, "Thou shall not commit adultery."
"Not commit adultery?   We're not interested", they replied
Finally, He went to the Jews and said, "I have some Commandments."
"Commandments?"   They said, "How much are they?"
"They're free," said God.
"We'll take 10!"

Blondes

Blonde - A light haired detour on the information super highway.

Q. What did the blonde say, when told she was pregnant?
A. Is it mine?

Q. Why did the blonde keep running out to her mail box?
A. Because her computer told her "She had mail"

Q. How do you tell if a blonde is using the computer?
A. Because of all the white out on the screen.

Q. What do you call 10 blondes lined up shoulder-to-shoulder?
A. A wind tunnel.

Q. What did the blonde say after having sex?
A. Goooo team!

Q. How do you get a blond out of a tree?
A. Wave.

Q. What do you get when you turn 3 blondes upside-down?
A. Two brunettes.

Q. Why did the blonde keep a coat hanger in her back seat?
A. In case she locks the keys in her car.

Q. How do you confuse a blonde?
A. Tell her to alphabetize a bag of M&M's.

Q. Why can't blondes put in light bulbs?
A. They keep breaking them with the hammers.

Q. What is black and hangs from the ceiling?
A. A blonde electrician.

Q. Why is a blonde like a door knob?
A. Because everybody gets a turn.

Q. What do you call a smart blonde?
A. A golden retriever.

Q. How do you drown a blonde?
A. Put a scratch 'n sniff card at the bottom of a pool.

A blonde was out hiking in the woods and came across a lake.
She spotted another blonde on the other side.
Yelling out to her she asked, "How do you get to the other side?"
The other blonde yelled back, "This is the other side!"

Two blondes were walking along the beach when one of them shouted, "Look,
a dead bird!"
The other one looked up at the sky and said, "Where"?

Did you hear about the blonde who wanted a bigger oven because she wanted
to make her husband some chocolate moose for dinner.

A young Redhead goes to the local urgent care medical office and says that her
body hurts wherever she touches it.
"Impossible", says the doctor. "Show me."
She takes her finger and pushes her elbow and screams in agony. She pushes
her knee and screams, pushes her ankle and screams.
The doctor says, "You're not really a redhead, are you?"
"No," she says, "I'm actually a Blonde."
"I thought so", the doctor says. "Your finger is broken."

Did you hear about the blonde who won a gold medal at the Olympics?
She took it home and had it bronzed.

2 blondes were talking and the first one says to the other, "Any idea what you
are getting from your husband for your birthday?"
The second one says, "Roses. That's a given."
The first one says, "What's wrong with that?"
The second one says, "Well he always has expectations after giving me flowers
and I don't feel like spending the next 3 days on my back with my legs in he
air."
The first one says, "Don't you have a vase?"

Did you hear about the blonde who stayed up all night studying for her urine
test?

---

3 blondes were asked to comment about a police profile sketch.
The first blonde says, "He only has 1 ear."
The police officer states, "It's a profile. You only see 1 side of the face."
The second blonde says, "He only has 1 eye."
The police officer again states, "It's a profile. There is only 1 side drawn."
The third blond states, "He must wear contact lenses."
The officer checks his file and says, "Yes, he does wear contact lenses. That's incredible. How did you know?"
The third blond says, "With only one ear and one eye, how would he keep glasses on?"

A Blonde is watching the news with her husband when the newscaster reports, "Two Brazilian men die in a skydiving accident."
The blonde starts crying to her husband, stating, "That's soo horrible!!
She turns to him and thru her tears asks, "How many is a Brazilian?"

A blonde was worried that her mechanic might try to rip her off.
She was relieved when he told her all she really needed was turn signal fluid.

Did you hear about the blonde who thought manual labor was the president of Mexico?

A blonde calls Delta Airlines and asks, "Can you tell me how long it'll take to fly from San Francisco to New York City?"
The agent replies," Just a minute…"
'Thank you," the blonde says, and hangs up.

A guy took his blonde girlfriend to her first football game. They had great seats right behind their team's bench. After the game, he asked her how she liked the it.
"Oh, I really liked it," she replied, "especially the tight pants and all the big muscles, but I just couldn't understand why they were killing each other over 25 cents!"
Dumbfounded, he asked, "What do you mean?"
"Well, they flipped a coin, one team got it and then for the rest of the game, all they kept screaming was: 'Get the quarterback! Get the quarterback!'
I'm like...Helloooooooooooooo? It's only 25 cents!!!!!!"

A redhead, brunette and a blonde were about to be executed.
The guard brings the redhead out to the firing line and ask her if she has any last words.
She says no.
So the guard commences, with "Ready… Aim…"
The redhead yells "Earthquake."
As everybody ducks for cover, she escapes.
The guard then brings the brunette out to the firing line, and ask if she has any last words.
She also says no.
So the guard commences, with "Ready… Aim…"
The brunette yells "Tornado."
As everybody hits the ground, the brunette escapes as well.
The blonde seeing all this thinks she also has a way to escape.
The guard brings the blonde out to the firing line and ask if she has any last words.
She says no.
So the guard commences, with "Ready… Aim…"
The blonde yells "Fire."

A blonde was shopping and came across a shiny silver thermos. She was quite fascinated by it so she took it to the sales clerk and asked what it was.
The clerk said, "It's a thermos. It keeps hot things hot and cold things cold."
"Wow", said the blonde. "I'm going to buy it!"
So she buys the thermos and takes it to work the next day.
A co-worker sees it and asks "What's that?"
"Why that's a thermos. It keeps hot things hot and cold things cold," the blonde replies.
"What do you have in it?" the co-worker asked.
"Two popsicles and some coffee."

Sign in a restaurant owned by a blonde:
"Open 7 days a week and weekends too."

A blonde goes over to her friend's house wearing a 'T.G.I.F.' t-shirt.
The friend asks, "Why are you wearing a 'Thank God It's Friday t-shirt on Monday?"
The blonde replies, "Oh, I thought it meant. 'This Goes In Front'"

After becoming very frustrated with the attitude of one of the Florida shopkeepers, the young blonde declared," Well, then, maybe I'll just go out and catch my own alligator and get a pair of alligator shoes for free!"
The shopkeeper replied with a sly smile, "Well, little lady, why don't you just give it a try. I'd like to see that."
The blonde heads off to the swamp, determined to catch an alligator.
The next day, as the shopkeeper was driving home, he spotted the same young woman standing waist deep in the murky water, with a shotgun in hand.
As he brought his car to a stop, he saw a huge 9-foot alligator swimming towards her.
With lightning quick reflexes, the blond takes aim and shoots the creature dead. Then she proceeds to haul it up onto the embankment. Right nearby were 5 more dead alligators, all lying belly up. The shopkeeper stood on the bank, watching in silent amazement as the blonde struggled and finally managed to flip the alligator onto its back.
Looking down, she screams in frustration, "Damn. This one's barefoot too!"

A blonde woman says to her husband," I'm having some trouble with the car. I think there's water in the carburetor."
Her husband states," Water in the carburetor? That's ridiculous!"
The blonde replies," I tell you there is water in the carburetor."
The husband asks her," You don't even know what a carburetor is. Where's the car?"
The blonde replies, "In the pool."

Blonde's Diary on a Cruise Ship
Day 1:
All packed for the cruise ship - all my sexiest dresses and make-up. Really excited.
Day 2:
Entire day at sea, beautiful and saw whales and dolphins. Met the Captain today - seems like a very nice man.
Day 3:
Ran into the Captain at the pool today and he invited me to join him at his table for dinner. Felt honored and had a wonderful time. He is very attractive and attentive.
Day 4:
Captain asked me to have dinner with him in his own cabin. Had a luxurious meal complete with caviar and champagne. He told me if I did not let him have his way with me he would sink the ship.
Day 5:
Today I saved 1,600 lives. Twice.

A girl was visiting her blonde friend, who had acquired two new dogs, and asked her what their names were.

The blonde responded by saying that one was named Rolex and one was named Timex. Her friend said," Whoever heard of someone naming dogs like that?" "HELLLOOOOOOO......,"answered the blond. "They're watch dogs!"

An attractive blonde arrived at the casino. She seemed a little intoxicated and bet twenty-thousand dollars on a single roll of the dice.

She said, "I hope you don't mind, but I feel much luckier when I'm completely nude."

With that, she stripped from the neck down, rolled the dice and with and yelled, "Come on, baby, Mama needs new clothes!"

As the dice came to a stop, she jumped up and down and squealed, "YES, YES! I WON!"

She hugged each of the dealers, then picked up her winnings and clothes and departed.

The dealers stared at each other dumbfounded.

Finally, one of them asked, "What did she roll?"

The other answered, "I don't know - I thought you were watching."

A blonde called the technical help line and asked, "Can you give me the extension number of Jack?"

The technician says, "I'm sorry, but there is no Jack here."

The blonde says, "There must be. Can you give me the extension number of Jack?"

The technician says, "I'm sorry but I don't understand."

The blonde continues, "But it says so right here. On page 5 of the manual, 'that I need to unplug from the wall socket and telephone jack'. Now can you give me his extension?"

A blonde goes to an appliance store and shows the clerk which TV she wants. The clerk tells her they don't do business with blondes. Insulted and angry, she goes home and dyes her hair black. The next day, she goes back to the appliance store, gets the clerk, and points to the TV she wants.

The clerk replies with , "Sorry, we don't do business with blondes."

The blonde is startled and asks, How did you know I am a blonde?"

The clerk replies, "Because you are pointing to a microwave."

During a password check, a blonde was found using the following password: 'MickeyMinniePlutoHueyLouieDeweyDonaldGoofy'.

When asked why it her password was so big.

The blonde replied, "The instructions said it had to be at least 8 characters long.

A blonde dies and goes to Heaven.

She is at the Pearly Gates, met by St. Peter himself. However, the gates are closed, and the blonde approaches the St Peter.

St. Peter said, "Well, it is certainly good to see you. We have heard a lot about you. I must tell you, though, that the place is filling up fast, and we have been administering an entrance examination for everyone. The test is short, but you have to pass it before you can get into Heaven."

The blonde responds, "It sure is good to be here, St. Peter, sir. But nobody ever told me about any entrance exam. I sure hope that the test isn't too hard. Life was a big enough test as it was." St. Peter continued, "Yes, I know, but the test is only three questions.

"First question: What two days of the week begin with the letter T?

Second question: How many seconds are there in a year?

Third question: What is God's first name?"

The blonde leaves to think the questions over. She returns the next day and sees St. Peter, who waves her over.

He says, "Now that you have had a chance to think over the questions, what are the answers."

The blonde replied, "Well, the first one-which two days in the week begins with the letter 'T'? That one is easy. That would be Today and Tomorrow."

The Saint's eyes opened wide and he exclaimed, "That is not what I was thinking, but you do have a point, and I guess I did not specify, so I will give you credit for that answer." "Now what about the next one?" asked St. Peter, "How many seconds in a year?"

"Now that one is a little harder," replied the blonde, "but I thought about it and I guess the only answer can be twelve."

Astounded, St. Peter said, "Twelve? How in Heaven's name could you come up with twelve seconds in a year?"

The blonde replied, "There's got to be twelve: January 2nd, February 2nd, March 2nd... "

'Hold it,' interrupts St. Peter, "I see where you are going with this, and I see your point, though that was not quite what I had in mind....but I will have to give you credit for that one, too. Let us go on with the third and final question. Can you tell me God's first name?"

"Sure," the blonde replied, "it's Andy."

"Andy?", exclaimed an exasperated and frustrated St Peter.

'"Ok, I can understand how you came up with your answers to my first two questions, but just how in the world did you come up with the name Andy as the first name of God?"

"That was the easiest one of all," the blonde replied. "'I learned it from that song; 'Andy walks with me, Andy talks with me, Andy tells me I am his own'."

A blonde worker was feeling stressed and needed to take some time off, but knew her boss would not allow her to leave. She thought if she acted crazy, he would tell her to take a few days off. So she hung upside down from the ceiling and made buzzing noises.

When her boss walked in saw her and asked , "What in God's name are you doing?"

She said, "I am a light bulb."

The boss said, "You are clearly stressed out. Go home and recuperate for a couple of days."

She jumped down and walked out of the office.

Another blonde co-worker started follow the first one leaving.

The boss asked her, "And where do you think you are going?"

The blonde replied, "I'm going home too, I can't work in the dark."

A blonde goes out for some drinks with her friends. She's had a bit too much to drink and on the ride home she is swerving a bit. A police officer sees and pulls her over. As he his questioning her, he smells the alcohol and has her submit to a breathalyzer test.

She does. When she is finished, the officer looks at the reading and states, "Well, it looks like you've had a couple of stiff ones."

To which the blonde replies, "It can tell you that too!"

A blonde was crossing a street with her boyfriend. The stoplight on the corner buzzes when it's safe to cross the street. He asked her if she knew what the buzzer was for.

When she said she didn't know, he explained that it signals to blind people when the light is red.

Appalled, she responded, "What on earth are blind people doing driving?!"

A blonde was taking her dress to the cleaners to get a stain removed.

The clerk didn't understand her and said, "Come again?"

The blonde replied, "No it was mustard."

In a semi rural area a blonde called the local city office to request the removal of the DEER CROSSING sign on the road by her house.

She explained. "Too many deer are being hit by cars out here! I don't think this is a good place for them to be crossing anymore. Couldn't you put the sign somewhere else?"

A girl went to a local Taco Bell and ordered a taco.

She asked the blonde behind the counter for "minimal lettuce."

She said she was sorry, but they only had 'Iceberg' lettuce.

A blonde was checking in at the airport gate when a security employee asked her, "Has anyone put anything in your baggage without your knowledge?" To which she replied, "If it was without my knowledge, how would I know?"

A veteran, trying to use the G.I. Bill for college courses, was enrolling in 15 college credits. When he went up to the registration counter, a blonde was working and told the vet he didn't qualify because he needed to be enrolled in 12 credits to be eligible.

A blonde plugged her power strip back into itself and couldn't understand why her system would not turn on.

Old Age

An 85-year-old man was asked by his doctor for a sperm count as part of his physical exam.

The doctor gave the man a jar and said, "Take this jar home and bring back a semen sample tomorrow."

The next day the 85-year-old man reappeared at the doctor's office and gave him the jar, which was as clean and empty as on the previous day.

The doctor asked what happened and the man explained," Well, doc, it's like this - first I tried with my right hand, but nothing. Then I tried with my left hand, but still nothing. Then I asked my wife for help. She tried with her right hand, then with her left, still nothing. She tried with her mouth, first with the teeth in, then with her teeth out, still nothing. We even called up the lady next door and she tried too. First with both hands, then an arm pit, and she even tried squeezin' it between her knees, but still nothing.

The doctor was shocked! "You asked your neighbor?"

The old man replied, "Yep, none of us could get the jar open."

An old man in his mid-eighties struggles to get up from the couch puts on his coat.

His wife, seeing the unexpected behavior asks, "Where are you going?"

He replies, "I'm going to the doctor."

She says, "Why, are you sick?"

He says, "Nope, I'm going to get me some of that Viagra stuff."

Immediately the wife starts working and positioning herself to get out of her rocker and begins to put on her coat.

He says, "Where the heck are you going"?

She answers, "I'm going to the doctor, too."

He says, "Why, what do you need?"

She says, "If you're going to start using that rusty old thing, I'm getting a Tetanus shot."

Two guys, one old and one young, are pushing their carts around Home Depot when they collide. The old guy says to the young guy, "Sorry about that. I'm looking for my wife and I guess I wasn't paying attention to where I was going."

The young guy says, "That's OK. It's a coincidence. I'm looking for my wife, too. I can't find her and I'm getting a little desperate."

The old guy says, "Well, maybe we can help each other. What does your wife look like?"

The young guy says, "Well, she is 27 years old, tall, with red hair, blue eyes, long legs, and large breasts... oh... and she's wearing tight white shorts. What does your wife look like?"

The old guy says, "Doesn't matter... Let's look for yours!"

There are 2 ways to tell you are getting old.
The second is your memory starts to go, and I can't remember the first.

An 86-year-old man walked into a crowded waiting room and approached the desk.
The receptionist cheerfully said, "Hello, sir. Can you please tell me why you're here to see the doctor today?"
"There's something wrong with my dick," he replied.
The receptionist became irritated and said, "You shouldn't come into a crowded waiting room and say something like that."
"Why not? You asked me what was wrong and I told you," he said.
The receptionist irritatingly replied, "Now you've caused some embarrassment in this room full of people. You should have said there is something wrong with your ear or something and discussed the problem further with the doctor in private."
The man replied, "You shouldn't ask people questions in a room full of strangers, if the answer could embarrass anyone."
The man walked out, waited several minutes and then re-entered.
The receptionist smiled smugly and asked, "Yes?"
"There's something wrong with my ear," he stated.
The receptionist nodded approvingly and smiled, knowing he had taken her advice.
"And what is wrong with your ear, sir?" she asked.
"I can't piss out of it," he replied.

A couple had been married for 50 years.
They were sitting at the breakfast table one morning when the wife says,
"Just think, fifty years ago we were sitting here at this breakfast table together."
"I know. We were probably sitting here naked as a jaybird fifty years ago." said the man.
"Well," Granny snickered. "Let's relive some old times."
Where upon, the two stripped to the buff and sat down at the table.
"You know, honey," the little old lady breathlessly replied, "My nipples are as hot for you today as they were fifty years ago."
"I wouldn't be surprised," he says "One's in your coffee and the other is in your oatmeal."

An old man goes into a drug store to buy some Viagra.
"Can I have 6 Viagra tablets, cut in quarters?" he asks.
" I can cut them for you", says the pharmacist, "but a quarter tablet will not give you a full erection."
"I'm 96," says the old man, "I don't want an erection. I just want it sticking out far enough so I don't pee on my slippers."

A teenage granddaughter comes downstairs for her date wearing a blouse that was semi-see-through and no bra. Her grandmother just about dies of shock. "Don't you DARE go out like that!" she scolded.

The teenager tells her, "Loosen up Grams. These are modern times. You gotta let your rose buds show." And out she went. The next day the teenager comes down the stairs and the Grandmother is sitting there with no top on. Now the teenager just about dies of shock. She explains to her grandmother that she has friends coming over and that it is just not appropriate.

The grandmother says, "Loosen up sweetie. If you can show off your rose buds, then I can display my hanging gardens."

An old prospector shuffled into town leading an old tired mule.

The old man headed straight for the only saloon in town to clear his parched throat.

He walked up to the saloon and tied his old mule to the hitch rail.

As he stood there brushing some of the dust from his face and clothes, a young gunslinger stepped out of the saloon with a gun in one hand and a bottle of whiskey in the other.

The young gunslinger looked at the old man and laughed, saying, "Hey old man, have you ever danced?"

The old man looked up at the gunslinger and said, "No, I never did dance, -- just never wanted to."

A crowd had gathered quickly and the gunslinger grinned and said, "Well, you old fool, you're gonna' dance now," and started shooting at the old man's feet.

The old prospector in order to not get a toe blown off or his boots perforated was soon hopping around like a flea on a hot skillet and everybody was laughing fit to be tied.

When the last bullet had been fired, the young gunslinger, still laughing, holstered his gun and turned around to go back into the saloon.

The old man turned to his pack mule, pulled out a double barreled shotgun, and cocked both hammers back. The loud, audible double clicks carried clearly through the desert air.

The crowd stopped laughing immediately. The young gunslinger heard the sounds too, and he turned around very slowly. The quiet was almost deafening.

The crowd watched as the young gunman stared at the old timer and the large gaping holes of those twin barrels. He found it hard to swallow. The barrels of the shotgun never wavered in the old man's hands.

The old man said, "Son, did you ever kiss a mule's ass?"

The boy bully swallowed hard and said, "No. But I've always wanted to."

An old married couple made a deal that whoever dies first would come back and inform the other of the afterlife. Their biggest fear was that there was no afterlife at all.

After a long life together, the husband was to first to go. True to his word, he made first contact: "Maude... Maude"

"Is that you Bill?" she asked.

"Yes, I've come back like we agreed..."

"That's great. What's it like?"

"Well, I get up in the morning, I make whoopee. I have breakfast and then it's off to the golf course. I make whoopee again, bathe in the warm sun and make whoopee a couple of more times. Then I have lunch, lots of greens, then another romp around the golf course, then pretty much make whoopee the rest of the afternoon. I catch some much needed sleep and then the next day, it starts all over again."

"Oh, you must be in heaven?" she asked.

"Well not exactly, I'm a rabbit on a golf course in Arizona."

Two old guys were chatting. One said to the other, "Yesterday was my 85th birthday. My wife gave me an SUV."

The other guy responded, "Wow, that's amazing. An SUV! What a great gift!"

The first guy said, "Yup! Socks, Underwear and Viagra!"

On a mans 72nd birthday, he got a gift certificate from his wife for a visit to a medicine man living on a reservation who was rumored to have a wonderful cure for erectile dysfunction. The man went to the reservation handed the ticket to the medicine man and wondered what would happen next.

The medicine man produced a potion, handed it to the man and said, "This is a powerful medicine and it must be respected. You take a teaspoonful and then say '1-2-3'. When you do that, you will become more manly than you have ever been in your life and you can perform as long as you want.

The man was encouraged and asked, "How do you stop the medicine from working?"

The medicine man replied, "Your partner must say 1-2-3-4. But when she does, the medicine will not work again until the next full moon."

The man was very excited, went home and took a spoonful of the potion, then invited his wife to join him in the bedroom.

When she came in, he took off his clothes and said,"1-2-3."

Immediately, he was the manliest of men.

The wife started taking her clothes off and asked, "What was the '1-2-3' for?

A lonely 70 year old widow decided that it was time to put an add in the paper that read:

'Husband Wanted:

Must be in my age group (70's)

Must not beat me

Must not run around on me

Must still be good in bed

Apply in person'

The next day she heard the doorbell rang, When she answered it, much to her dismay, she saw a grey-haired gentleman sitting in a wheelchair with no arms and no legs.

"I'm here to answer the ad", he said.

The old woman looked at him and said, "You're not seriously asking me to consider you are you? Look at you, you have no legs!"

The old man smiled and said, "Ten, I cannot run around on you!"

She replied, "You don't have any arms either!"

He replied, "Therefore, I can never beat you, either."

The old woman raised an eyebrow and asked, "Are you still good in bed?"

The old man leaned back and with a big smile said, "Rang the doorbell, didn't I?"

An elderly couple had dinner at another couple's house and after eating, the wives left the table and went into the kitchen.

The two men were talking and one said, "Last night we went out to a new restaurant and it was really great. I would recommend it very highly."

The other man asked, "What is the name of the restaurant?"

The first man though a second and finally said, "What is the name of that flower you give to someone you love? The one that is red and has thorns."

The second man said, "Do you mean a rose?"

The first man said, "Yes, that's the one." He then yelled out to the kitchen, "Rose, what's the name of the restaurant we went to last night?"

A woman asks her husband, "Would you like some breakfast, maybe some bacon and eggs, or some toast. or coffee?"

He replies, "Thanks, but I'm not that hungry. The Viagra has taken the edge off my appetite."

Later she asks, "Would you like a sandwich or some soup?"

He again replies, "No thanks. That Viagra really killed my desire for any food"

At dinnertime, she asks him, "Do you want anything to eat? How about a nice steak, or chicken?"

Once again he states, "Still not hungry, It's got to be the Viagra."

She finally says, "Well will you let me up, I'm starving."

A group of retired Americans were taking a tour bus through Holland. As they came upon a cheese farm, the young tour guide explained the process of making cheese, explaining all about the goat's milk and how it was used. He then showed the group a hillside where many goats were grazing.

The guide explained, "Here are the older goats. We put them out to pasture when they can no longer produce. What do you Americans do with your old goats?"

An old man yelled out, "They send us out on bus tours!"

The couple was 85 years old and had been married for sixty years. Though they were far from rich, they managed to get by because they watched their pennies. Though not young, they were both in very good health, largely due to the wife's insistence on healthy foods and exercise for the last decade.

One day, their good health didn't help when they went on a rare vacation and their plane crashed, sending them off to Heaven.

They reached the pearly gates, and St. Peter escorted them inside. He took them to a beautiful mansion, furnished in gold and fine silks, with a fully stocked kitchen and a waterfall in the master bath. A maid could be seen hanging their favorite clothes in the closet.

They gasped in astonishment when he said, "Welcome to Heaven. This will be your home now."

The old man asked Peter, "How much is all this going to cost?"

"Why, nothing," Peter replied, "Remember, this is your reward in Heaven."

The old man looked out the window and right there he saw a championship golf course, finer and more beautiful than any ever built on Earth.

"What are the greens fees?" grumbled the old man.

'This is heaven,' St. Peter replied. "You can play for free, every day."

Next they went to the clubhouse and saw the lavish buffet lunch, with every imaginable cuisine laid out before them, from seafood to steaks to exotic deserts, free flowing beverages.

"Don't even ask," said St. Peter. "This is Heaven, it is all free for you to enjoy."

The old man looked around and glanced nervously at his wife.

"Where are the low fat and low cholesterol foods and the decaffeinated tea?" he asked.

"That's the best part,' St. Peter replied. 'You can eat and drink as much as you like of whatever you like and you will never get fat or sick. This is Heaven!"

The old man pushed, "No gym to work out at?"

"Not unless you want to," was the answer.

"No testing my sugar or blood pressure or...?"

"Never again. All you do here is enjoy yourself," was that answer.

The old man glared at his wife and said, "You and your damn bran Flakes. We could have been here ten years ago!"

An elderly couple were celebrating their 50th anniversary. The couple had married as high school sweethearts and had still lived in the same neighborhood.

They walked back to their old school, found it wasn't locked and found his desk where he had carved their initials in a heart.

Walking home hand in hand, a bag of money fell out of an armored car landing at their feet. The old woman picked up the bag and they took it home. Once back home, she counted it and found it contained twenty five thousand dollars. Her husband said, "We should give it back."

He replied, "Finders keepers", put the money back in the bag and hid it in the attic.

A few days later two FBI men were searching the neighborhood looking for the money.

They knocked on the old couples door and asked, "Did either one of you find a bag that fell out of an armored car yesterday?"

The old lady replied, "No."

The old man states, "She's lying. She hid it up in the attic."

The wife then states, "Oh you can't believe anything he says, he's going senile."

The agents turn to the husband, take out their notebooks and state, "Why don't you tell us everything that happened. Start from the beginning."

The old man starts, "Well, it all started when me and my wife were walking home from school yesterday..."

You know you are getting old when:

It's harder to tell navy from black!

Your kids are becoming you, and you don't like them, but your grandchildren are perfect!

Yellow becomes the big color...walls...hair...teeth!

The candles on the cake cost more than the cake.

Going out is good. Coming home is better!

When people say you look "Great"...they add "for your age"!

The best thing about getting old is the discounts.

You forget names...but it's OK because other people forgot they even knew you.

The last 2 outfits you wore had spots on them.

The five pounds you wanted to lose is now 15 and you have a better chance of losing your keys than the 15 pounds.

Instead of wearing clean underwear in case you GET in an accident, now you bring clean underwear in case you do HAVE an accident!

You miss the days when everything worked with just an "ON" and "OFF" switch.

You use more 4 letter words..."what?"..."when?"

Now that you can afford expensive jewelry, it's not safe to wear it anywhere.

Many of the people in People Magazine you've never heard of...

You don't have hair under your arms and very little on your legs but your chin needs to be plucked daily!

What used to be freckles are now liver spots.

Everybody whispers.

You bend down to tie your shoes, and wonder what else you can do down there.

You have 3 sizes of clothes in your closet, 2 of which you will never wear again

Your birthday suit needs pressing.

Your hear your favorite song on the elevator.

Your the one calling the police on the kids with their loud music.

Everything either dries up or leaks.

Your back goes out more than you do.

You chase woman, but its only downhill.

It takes all night to do what you used to do all night.

You remember when a program meant something on TV, an application was something you filled out, and a CD was something from the bank.

You go out for a night on the town and are home by 9:00 pm.

Getting a little action' means you don't need any fiber today.

You get the same sensation from a rocking chair as a roller coaster.

You don't care where your spouse goes, just as long as you don't have to go along.

You car insurance goes down because of your age, but your health insurance goes up.

Children

She was in the bathroom, putting on her makeup, under the watchful eyes of her young granddaughter as she'd done many times before.
After she applied her lipstick and started to leave, the little one said, "But Gramma, you forgot to kiss the toilet paper good-bye!"

A young grandson called his grandmother to wish her a Happy Birthday.
He asked me how old she was, and she told him, "62."
He was quiet for a moment, and then he asked, "Did you start at 1?"

After putting her grandchildren to bed, a grandmother changed into old slacks and a droopy blouse and proceeded to wash her hair. As she heard the children getting more and more rambunctious, her patience grew thin. Finally, she threw a towel around her head and stormed into their room, putting them back to bed with stern warnings. As she left the room, she heard the 3-year-old say with a trembling voice, "Who was THAT?"

A grandmother was telling her little granddaughter what her own childhood was like: "We used to skate outside on a pond. I had a swing made from a tire; it hung from a tree in our front yard. We rode our pony. We picked wild raspberries in the woods." The little girl was wide-eyed, taking this all in. At last she said, "I sure wish I'd gotten to know you sooner!"

A grandson was visiting his grandmother one day when he asked, "Grandma, do you know how you and God are alike?",
"No, how are we alike?" the grandmother replied.
"You're both old," he replied.

A little girl was diligently pounding away on her grandfather's word processor. She told him she was writing a story.
"What's it about?" he asked.
"I don't know," she replied. "I can't read."

A grandson asked his grandfather how old he was, the grandfather teasingly replied, "I'm not sure how old I am."
"Look in your underwear, Grandpa," he advised. "Mine says I'm four to six."

A second grader came home from school and said to her grandmother, "Grandma, guess what? We learned how to make babies today."
The grandmother, more than a little surprised, tried to keep her cool. "That's interesting," she said, "how do you make babies?"
"It's simple," replied the girl. "You just change 'y' to 'I' and add 'es'."

"Give me a sentence about a public servant," asked a teacher.
The small boy wrote: "The fireman came down the ladder pregnant."
The teacher took the boy aside to ask him. "Do you know what pregnant means?"
"Sure," said the young boy confidently. "It means carrying a child."

A nursery school teacher was delivering a station wagon full of kids home one day when a fire truck zoomed past. Sitting in the front seat of the truck was a Dalmatian dog. The children started discussing the dog's duties. "They use him to keep crowds back," said one child.
"No," said another, "he's just for good luck."
A third child brought the argument to a close. "They use the dogs to find the fire hydrants."

A little girl was talking to her teacher about whales.
The teacher said it was physically impossible for a whale to swallow a human because even though it was a very large mammal its throat was very small. The little girl stated that Jonah was swallowed by a whale.
Irritated, the teacher reiterated that a whale could not swallow a human; it was physically impossible.
The little girl said, "When I get to heaven I will ask Jonah."
The teacher asked, "What if Jonah went to Hell?"
The little girl replied, "Then you ask him ."

A 6-year-old and 4-year-old brothers are upstairs in their bedroom.
"You know what?" says the 6-year-old. "I think it's about time we started cussin'."
The 4-year-old nods his head in approval. The 6-year-old continues: "When we go downstairs for breakfast, I'll say something with 'hell' and you say something with 'ass.'"
The 4-year-old agrees with enthusiasm.
When their mother walks into the kitchen and asks the 6-year-old what he wants for breakfast, he replies, "Aw, hell, mom... I guess I'll have some Cheerios."
Whack!! He flies out of his chair, tumbles across the kitchen floor, gets up and runs upstairs crying his eyes out with his mother in hot pursuit, slapping his rear on each step.
His mom locks him in his room and shouts, "You can stay in there until I let you out."
She then comes back downstairs, looks at the 4-year-old and asks with a stern voice, "And what do you want for breakfast, young man?"
"I don't know," he blubbers, "But you can bet your ass it won't be Cheerios!"

A teacher asked one of her students if he says prayers before eating a meal. The student replied, "No ma'am, I don't have to, my Mom is a good cook."

A Sunday school teacher was discussing the Ten Commandments with her five and six year olds. After explaining the commandment to "honor" thy Father and thy Mother, she asked, "Is there a commandment that teaches us how to treat our brothers and sisters?"
Without missing a beat one little boy answered, "Thou shall not kill."

One day a little girl was sitting and watching her mother do the dishes at the kitchen sink. She suddenly noticed that her mother had several strands of white hair sticking out in contrast on her brunette head.
She looked at her mother and asked, "Why are some of your hairs white, Mom?"
Her mother replied, "Well, every time that you do something wrong and make me cry or unhappy, one of my hairs turns white."
The little girl thought about this revelation for a while and then said, "Momma, how come ALL of grandma's hairs are white?"

Attending a wedding for he first time, a little girl whispered to her mother, "Why is the bride dressed in white?"
"Because white is the color of happiness, and today is the happiest day of her life."
The girl thought for a moment then said, "So why is the groom wearing black?"

A teacher was giving a lesson on the circulation of the blood. Trying to make the matter clearer, she said, "Now, class, if I stood on my head, the blood, as you know, would run into it, and I would turn red in the face."
"Yes," the class said.
"Then why is it that while I am standing upright in the ordinary position, the blood doesn't run into my feet?"
A little fellow shouted, "That's because your feet aren't empty."

The children were lined up in the cafeteria of a Catholic elementary school for lunch.
At the head of the table was a large pile of apples.
The nun made a note, and posted on the apple tray: "Take only ONE. God is watching."
Moving further along the lunch line, at the other end of the table was a large pile of chocolate chip cookies.
A child had written a note, "Take all you want. God is watching the apples."

A teacher asked the following questions of her students:
"What do you think your mom and dad have in common?"
The students replied, "Both don't want any more kids"
Teacher: "When is it okay to kiss someone?"
Student: "When they're rich."
Teacher: "How would the world be different if people didn't get   married?"
Student: "There sure would be a lot of kids to explain, wouldn't there?"

After a lengthy church service a little boy tells the pastor, "When I grow up, I'm going to give you some money."
"Well, thank you," the pastor replied, "but why?"
"Because my daddy says you're one of the poorest preachers we've ever had."

A Sunday school teacher was asking her students if anybody knew what God's name is.
One student said, "God's name is Howard."
The teacher wanted to know why he thought that.
The student said, "It says so in the Lords prayer. Our father who art in Heaven. Howard be thy name."

A husband and wife were in bed having sex when little Billy walked in on them.
Little Billy sees them and turns around and flees.
The husband tells his wife," Well, I better go talk to him and make sure that he is ok."
He gets out of bed, gets dresses and heads into his son's room.
Upon entering his son's room, he sees little Billy having sex with his grandmother.
Little Billy see his father and states, "Let's see how you feel when its *your* mother!"

A Sunday school teacher asked her children as they were on the way to church service,
"And why is it necessary to be quiet in church?"
One bright little girl replied, "Because people are sleeping."

A little boy was overheard praying:
"Lord, if you can't make me a better boy, don't worry about it. I'm having a real good time like I am."

After the christening of his baby brother in church, a little boy was sobbing all the way home in the back seat of the car.

His father asked him three times what was wrong.

Finally, the boy replied, "That preacher said he wanted us all brought up in a nice Christian home, but I want to stay with you guys."

A wife invited some people to dinner.

At the table, she turned to their six-year-old daughter and said, "Would you like to say the blessing?"

"I wouldn't know what to say," the girl replied.

"Just say what you hear Mommy say," the wife answered.

The daughter bowed her head and said, "Lord, why on earth did I invite all these people to dinner?"

A small boy was wandering around lost at a large shopping mall.

He approached a uniformed policeman and said, "I've lost my grandpa!"

The cop asked, "What's he like?"

The little boy hesitated for a moment and then replied, "Crown Royal whiskey and women with big breasts."

The Head Start teacher asked a 4-year old, "What does your Daddy do?"

"He works in a paper mill", the boy replied.

"That's a good way to make money", the teacher said.

"He doesn't make money," the boy replied, "he makes toilet paper.

A little boy is out walking in the woods with his father when they come across 2 dogs screwing.

The boy turns to his father and asks, "Daddy, what are they doing?"

The father explains, "They are making puppies."

The boy seems to understand and they continue their outing and head home.

Late that night, the boy is in bed and wakes up from a bad dream.

He runs into his parent's room, and sees his parents screwing.

The boy asks his father, "Daddy, what are you doing?"

The father explains, "We are making a little brother or sister for you."

The boy replies, "Well turn her over, I want a puppy!"

A first-grade teacher, Ms. Brooks, was having trouble with one of her students. The teacher asked, "Harry, what's your problem?"

Harry answered, "I'm too smart for the 1st grade. My sister is in the 3rd grade and I'm smarter than she is! I think I should be in the 3rd grade too!"

Ms. Brooks had enough. She took Harry to the principal's office.

While Harry waited in the outer office, the teacher explained to the principal the situation. The principal told Ms. Brooks he would give the boy a test. If he failed to answer any of his questions, he was to go back to the 1st grade and behave. She agreed.

Harry was brought in, the conditions were explained to him and he agreed to take the test.

Principal: "What is 3 x 3?"

Harry: "9."

Principal: "What is 6 x 6?"

Harry: "36."

And so it went with every question the principal thought a 3rd grader should know.

The principal looks at Ms. Brooks and tells her, "I think Harry can go to the 3rd grade."

Ms. Brooks says to the principal, "Let me ask him some questions."

The principal and Harry both agreed.

Ms. Brooks asks, "What does a cow have four of that I have only two of?"

Harry, after a moment: "Legs."

Ms Brooks: "What is in your pants that you have but I do not have?"

The principal wondered why she'd ask such a question!

Harry replied: "Pockets."

Ms. Brooks: "What does a dog do that a man steps into?"

Harry: "Pants."

Ms. Brooks: What starts with a C, ends with a T, is hairy, oval, delicious, and contains thin, whitish liquid?"

Harry: "Coconut."

The principal sat forward with his mouth hanging open.

Ms. Brooks: "What goes in hard and pink & comes out soft and sticky?"

The principal's eyes opened really wide and before he could stop the answer.

Harry replied, "Bubble gum."

Ms. Brooks: "What does a man do standing up, a woman does sitting down and a dog does on three legs?"

Harry: "Shake hands."

The principal was trembling.

Ms. Brooks: "What word starts with an 'F' and ends in 'K' that means a lot of heat and excitement?"

Harry: "Fire truck."

The principal breathed a sigh of relief and told the teacher:

"Put Harry in the 5th grade, I got the last seven questions wrong."

Little Tony was 7 years old and was staying with his grandmother for a few days.

He'd been playing outside with the other kids for a while when he came into the house and asked her: "Grandma, what's that called when two people sleep in the same room and one is on top of the other?"

She was a little taken aback, but she decided to tell him the truth. "It's called sex, dear."

Little Tony said, "Oh, OK," and went back outside to play with the other kids. A few minutes later he came back in and said angrily, "Grandma, it isn't called sex.

It's called Bunk Beds! And Jimmy's mom wants to talk to you."

A mother is driving her little girl to her friend's house for a play date.

" Mommy," the little girl asks, "how old are you?"

"Honey, you are not supposed to ask a lady her age," the mother replied. "It's not polite."

"OK", the little girl says,

"How much do you weigh?"

"Now really," the mother says, "those are personal questions and are really none of your business."

Undaunted, the little girl asks, "Why did you and Daddy get a divorce?"

'That's enough questions, young lady! Honestly!"

The exasperated mother walks away as the two friends begin to play.

"My Mom won't tell me anything about her," the little girl says to her friend.

"Well," says the friend, "all you need to do is look at her driver's license. It's like a report card, it has everything on it."

Later that night the little girl says to her mother," I know how old you are. You are 32."

The mother is surprised and asks," How did you find that out?"

"I also know that you weigh 130 pounds..."

The mother is past surprised and shocked now.

"How in Heaven's name did you find that out?" she asks.

"And," the little girl says triumphantly," I know why you and daddy got a divorce."

"Oh really?" the mother asks. "Why?"

"Because you got an 'F' in sex."

DJ-age 4, stepped onto the bathroom scale and asked: "How much do I cost?"

Jack - age 3, was watching his Mom breast-feeding his new baby sister.

After a while he asked: "Mom why have you got two? Is one for hot and one for cold milk?"

A second grade teacher was trying to get her children to remember her name. She said to them, "My name is Miss Prussy. It sounds like pussy, only there's an 'R' in it.

When you go home today, try to remember it. Tomorrow I'll ask you what my name is"

The next day she asked her class, "Ok, who remembers my name? I will give you a hint.

It sounds like pussy, only there's an 'R' in it".

A little boy in the front row said, "Is it Miss Crunt?"

A first grade teacher was trying to teach her kids the different flavors associated with the different colors of a pack of life savers.

Red was cherry, yellow was lemon, orange was orange, green was lime, etc.

When she handed out the honey flavored life savers, none of her students knew what flavor it was.

She finally thought of something that might help, and told her class, "I'll give you all a clue. It's what your mother sometimes calls your father."

To which one of the little girls spit out the life saver saying, "Were eating assholes!"

Melanie -age 5, asked her Granny how old she was.

Granny replied she was so old she didn't remember any more.

Melanie said, "If you don't remember you must look in the back of your panties. Mine say five to six."

Steven -age 3, hugged and kissed his Mom good night. "I love you so much that when you die I'm going to bury you outside my bedroom window."

Brittany-age 4, had an ear ache and wanted a pain killer. She tried in vain to take the lid off the bottle. Seeing her frustration, her Mom explained it was a child-proof cap and she'd have to open it for her.

Eyes wide with wonder, the little girl asked: "How does it know it's me?"

Susan -age 4, was drinking juice when she got the hiccups. "Please don't give me this juice again," she said, "It makes my teeth cough."

Clinton -age 5, was in his bedroom looking worried when his Mom asked what was troubling him, he replied, "I don't know what'll happen with this bed when I get married. How will my wife fit in it?"

Marc -age 4, was engrossed in a young couple that were hugging and kissing in a public.
Without taking his eyes off them, he asked his dad: "Why is he whispering in her mouth?"

Tammy -age 4. was with her mother when they met an elderly, rather wrinkled woman her Mom knew.
Tammy looked at her for a while and then asked, "Why doesn't your skin fit your face?"

James -age 4,was listening to a Bible story. His dad read: 'The man named Lot was warned to take his wife and flee out of the city but his wife looked back and was turned to salt."
Concerned, James asked: "What happened to the flea?"

"Dear Lord," the minister began, with arms extended toward heaven and a rapturous look on his upturned face. "Without you, we are but dust..."
He would have continued but at that moment the obedient little four year old girl leaned over to asked quite audibly, "Mom, what is butt dust?"

A first grade teacher was testing her children to see if they understood how to get to heaven.
She asked them, "If I sold my house and my car and gave all the money to the church, would that get me into heaven?"
"No." the children replied.
"What if I cleaned the church every day, mowed the lawn and planted flowers? Would that get me into heaven?"
Again they replied, "No."
Then she asked, "What if I was kind to animals and gave candy to children? Would that get me into heaven?"
Once again they replied, "No."
She then asked, "Then how do I get to heaven?"
One boy shouted out, "You have to be dead first"

A father passing by his son's bedroom was astonished to see that his bed was nicely made and everything was picked up. Then he saw an envelope, propped up prominently on the pillow that was addressed to 'Dad.' With the worst premonition he opened the envelope with trembling hands and read the letter.

Dear Dad:
It is with great regret and sorrow that I'm writing you. I had to elope with my new girlfriend because I wanted to avoid a scene with Mom and you.
I have been finding real passion with Stacy and she is so nice.
But I knew you would not approve of her because of all her piercing, tattoos, tight motorcycle clothes and the fact that she is much older than I am.
But it' s not only the passion...Dad she's pregnant.
Stacy said that we will be very happy. She owns a trailer in the woods and has a stack of firewood for the whole winter. We share a dream of having many more children.
Stacy has opened my eyes to the fact that marijuana doesn't really hurt anyone. We'll be growing it for ourselves and trading it with the other people that live nearby for cocaine and ecstasy.
In the meantime we will pray that science will find a cure for AIDS so Stacy can get better. She deserves it.
Don't worry Dad. I'm 15 and I know how to take care of myself.
Someday I'm sure that we will be back to visit so that you can get to know your grandchildren.

Love, Your Son John

PS. Dad, none of the above is true. I'm over at Tommy's house.
I Just wanted to remind you that there are worse things in life than the Report card that is in my center desk drawer.

And this is the worst joke I have ever heard.

I was at a football game telling this one to a friend. When I finally finished the joke, he rolled up the program and hit me over the head with it.

The 'Tis bottle

There was a man who collected bottles. He had all sorts of bottles. Fat bottles, skinny bottles, tall bottles, square bottles, round bottles. Fat short bottles. Tall skinny bottles.
He had every type of bottle imaginable, except for one, the 'Tis bottle.
He heard that there were only 2 'Tis bottles left in existence and he searched all over for one to complete his collection.
In his search for the 'Tis bottle, he found that one was in the deepest part of the jungle and one was on the highest mountain of the Himalayas. So he charters and expedition to take him thru the deepest darkest parts of the jungle.
Thru the threes and foliage he goes. Foliage so thick, you could cut it with a knife or in his case a machete. And there it is, right in front of him, the long lost bottle to his collection sitting on a fallen tree. The 'Tis bottle.
But just as he is about to pick it up, a monkey climb down from the trees, grabs the bottle, climbs back up the tree and drops it, shattering it on some nearby rocks.
He goes home all dejected not being able to finally acquire the 'Tis bottle.
So he charters another expedition to take him up the highest mountain of the Himalayas.
He climbs, higher and higher thru the freezing wind, higher thru the cold, higher still thru the snow and ice. Higher at last until he is at the summit, the highest mountain of the Himalayas. And he sees it, the long lost bottle to his collection. The 'Tis bottle.
The very last one in existence.
Ecstatic he goes to grab it, but in the cold, the bottle is just too slick and slides from his hand, rolling down the mountain side.
A half frozen boulder jutting out of the snow catches the bottle at the last second before it slides off into oblivion.
He's got it. The 'Tis bottle! He is overjoyed. He puts it in a duffel bag to rush home.
He heads back down the mountain. He climbs down, lower and lower thru the snow and ice, lower thru the cold, lower still thru the freezing wind and heads home.
Finally arriving home he rushes into his house, runs into his kitchen and moves a rug away from his kitchen floor, exposing a trap door.
He opens the trap door, and goes down a dark stairwell.

He takes the stairs to an underground river, where there is a boat docked.
He gets in the boat and motors off down the river, coming to an underground vault.
He gets out of the boat and goes up to a vault.
He enters the combination to the vault, opens the door and he is in a room full of bottles.
All sorts of bottles. Fat bottles, skinny bottles, tall bottles, square bottles, round bottles. Fat short bottles. Tall skinny bottles. There is every type of bottle imaginable.
On one of the shelves, is an empty space.
The man takes the bottle out of the duffel bag, puts it on the empty space, picks up a spoon and while clinking the bottles with the spoon, sings "My coun-try

'*Tis* of thee."

Printed in Great Britain
by Amazon.co.uk, Ltd.,
Marston Gate.